ASSESSING
ACCESS

Towards a New
Social Union

ASSESSING
ACCESS

Towards a New Social Union

PROCEEDINGS OF THE
SYMPOSIUM ON THE
COURCHENE PROPOSAL

INSTITUTE OF
INTERGOVERNMENTAL
RELATIONS
QUEEN'S UNIVERSITY

Canadian Cataloguing in Publication Data

Symposium on the Courchene Proposal (1996 : Queen's University)
　　Assessing ACCESS : towards a new social union

Proceedings of a symposium held at Queen's University, Oct. 31-Nov. 1, 1996.
Includes bibliographical references.
ISBN 0-88911-591-5

1. Courchene, Thomas J., 1940–　. ACCESS : a convention on the Canadian economic and social systems – Congresses.　2. Canada – Economic policy – 1991–　– Congresses.* 3. Canada – Social policy – Congresses. 4. Canada – Politics and government – 1993–　– Congresses.* I. Queen's University (Kingston, Ont.). Institute of Intergovernmental Relations. II. Title.

HC115.S95 1996　　　338.971　　　C97-930793-7

Contents

PART THREE: COMMENTARY

APPENDIX

Acknowledgements

From its inception, this book has been a collaborative enterprise, and the Institute wishes to acknowledge the contribution of many individuals and institutions.

The project began as a symposium held by the Institute of Intergovernmental Relations at Queen's University, 31 October-1 November 1996. The symposium was organized because of the extensive interest sparked by Tom Courchene's paper on ACCESS (*A Convention on the Canadian Economic and Social Systems*).

The symposium brought together an impressive group of participants, including senior government officials from federal and provincial governments across Canada, and top academics in the area of intergovernmental relations. The discussions were thought-provoking, and vigorous debate was stimulated in analyzing the effectiveness of the ACCESS proposals, the necessary political dynamic for reform, and the influences that Courchene's two proposed models would have on Canadian federalism and democracy.

The organizers would like to acknowledge and thank the Governments of Ontario and New Brunswick for their financial support for this project.

The success of the symposium also depended heavily on the extensive planning and organizational support of the Institute of Intergovernmental Relations, and particular thanks are owed to Keith Banting, then Acting Director, Patti Candido, and Mary Kennedy. The preparation of the book itself once again reflects the professionalism of the Publication Unit in the School of Policy Studies. I wish to thank Valerie Jarus and Mark Howes for the production of camera-ready copy, and Marilyn Banting for copyediting.

Harvey Lazar
Kingston Ontario

PART ONE

RAPPORTEUR'S REPORT

Assessing ACCESS:
A Summary of Discussion

David Cameron

INTRODUCTION

The symposium brought government officials, academic researchers and policy commentators together to review and assess the proposals contained in Tom Courchene's ACCESS paper. The object was to better understand the implications of the models set out in the paper, and to assess their strengths and weaknesses. The paper sets out two models of the social union for Canada, an interim model and a full ACCESS model. The interim model includes a monitoring process and a dispute resolution mechanism, enforced by a federal-provincial agency or process; the full model relies on an interprovincial mechanism to sustain a pan-Canadian convention on social and economic programs.

OPENING REMARKS

Tom Courchene opened the symposium with some brief comments, as follows, on how his paper had been received in the many different fora in which he had participated:

- He was puzzled by the view of some commentators that the ACCESS approach would harm the economically weaker provinces. He pointed out that some people in the "have provinces" such as Alberta, have difficulty with the paper, too. How can both positions apply?

- He has difficulty with the charge that the approach would lead to fragmentation and decentralization. As he sees it, there is a lot of pan-Canadianism in the paper.

- While he has had relatively little contact with federal officials, he has received the following comments from that quarter: (i) the paper's approach would have been discarded out of hand two or three years ago, but there is more interest in it today, and (ii) the concrete proposals in the paper are helpful, because they make a better debate possible.

- The terminology in the paper (interim model and full ACCESS model) is unfortunate, because it appears to discourage a consideration of the modest proposal in its own right.

- The full model may be constraining and somewhat inflexible; it is clothed with too many principles.

- Several Quebecers averred that it is refreshing to see proposals for the major reform of federalism being fashioned in response to the needs of the country as a whole, rather than in response to pressures from Quebec. Indeed, Quebec is not even mentioned in the paper, yet its content is likely to appeal to soft nationalists in Quebec.

Tom concluded with the observation that there had so far been very little discussion of the second half of his paper, which deals with *compliance and enforcement* and with *monitoring and dispute resolution*.

DOES THE ACCESS APPROACH MAKE SENSE IN CANADA'S CURRENT SITUATION?

A good deal of the discussion during the symposium was devoted to considering whether the circumstances in which the country found itself called for the kind of approach on offer in the Courchene paper. Was it, or was it not, a case of a product meeting a market?

Conceptual Polarities

As the day proceeded, the conversation began implicitly to revolve around a number of conceptual polarities that participants used to articulate their views about the ACCESS proposals.

- incremental change versus comprehensive reform;

- policy simplicity versus design complexity;

- flexibility/untidiness versus coherence/rigidity;

- democratic/citizenship values versus intergovernmental processes;

- governmental agreements versus the courts;

- local options versus consolidated responsibility (pan-Canadian or Ottawa-based);

- market principles versus planned public outcomes.

About these polarities, there were conflicting views of two kinds: there was frequent disagreement about which side of a given polarity the Courchene paper actually fell on. This, a difference of interpretation as to the meaning of the report and its implications, was a continuation of the phenomenon Tom had reported on earlier. Second, there was also disagreement about the *desirability* of one polar orientation or the other. Some participants, for example, made a strong pitch for incremental reform, while others saw advantage in a more systematic approach.

Although no effort was made to assemble these polar orientations into different packages, there appeared to be a discernible tendency for people to cluster around one side of the list of polarities as indicated above or around the other.

Framework of Assumptions

Some participants questioned whether the framework of assumptions on which the ACCESS paper rested would withstand scrutiny. For example, the assumptions relating to:

- "Glocalization," the weakening of the nation state, as activity and authority migrates to the local and the supra-national level.

- The inevitability of continuing decentralization.

- The growing tension between north-south economic and trade links, and east-west social and political links.

- The continued dominance of deficit politics.

The Scope of the Paper

A number of participants expressed concern about the scope of the ACCESS proposals and asked whether such a comprehensive approach was feasible or desirable. One person put it this way: the package is too much like a non-constitutional version of the Charlottetown Accord. It was further noted that putting such a large set of proposals into effect would require an aggressive use of intergovernmental summitry, which would pose some challenges, given the country's present mood and circumstances. Those who expressed these views typically preferred an incremental, step-by-step approach, where adjustments could be made as necessary along the way.

A contrary view was expressed, however, arguing that a full package invests the proposals with weight and presence, which can be helpful if major change is contemplated.

The Fiscal Situation and Ottawa's Taste for Reform

Several people contended that it would be a mistake to get locked into a set of assumptions based on the belief that the fiscal pressures on Canadian governments would continue unabated. These people felt that it was necessary to envisage an era of post-deficit politics in which the public discourse, the perceived interests and ambitions of the federal and provincial governments, and the desires of the citizenry might be very different from what they are today. Alberta is already entering that new era, and Ottawa will not be very far behind.

Indeed, it is possible that the "window of opportunity" during which the federal government might be ready to embark on a major overhaul of the country in the direction indicated by the Courchene paper may be already closing or will close in the next two to five years; when Ottawa begins to sense that it has or will have some money in its pocket, its taste for the radical reform of its role in supporting the welfare state may disappear.

Quebec

One participant argued strongly that, although the Courchene proposals would constitute very substantial reform, they still only dealt with half the issue so far as Quebec was concerned. Yes, it was necessary to tackle the reform of the social and economic union, but it was also necessary to address the relationship between the two linguistic communities; Canada's national unity problems would not be solved in the absence of a settlement of Quebec's status in Confederation and the authoritative recognition of that status.

There was an acknowledgment that, at least in the short term, it could not be imagined that the current Government of Quebec would participate in the reconstruction of the social and economic union along Courchene lines. For some participants, this was wholly unacceptable, and meant that it would not be feasible to proceed. For a larger number of participants, this meant that the rest of the country could and should proceed without Quebec's involvement; needed improvements in the operation of the federation should not be held ransom to Quebec's current refusal to participate; making progress on this front would send a positive message to many people in Quebec, and Quebec could always sign on later when and if conditions changed.

A similar discussion occurred with respect to the question of whether and how one would proceed with some but not all of the other provinces.

Ontario

Several people, noting that the release of the ACCESS paper had occurred under the auspices of the Government of Ontario, underlined the fact that Ontario was now a major voice for reform of the federation. The province was now prepared to contemplate a degree of restructuring that would have been unthinkable a decade or so ago. Just as it was seeking higher levels of efficiency and effectiveness in governing structures and processes within the province, so it was prepared to put its weight behind a national effort to make the federation more effective. The fact that there has been policy continuity in this reformist impulse, despite changes of government, signalled the depth and solidity of this shift. In any analysis of the current situation, this was a factor that needed to be considered very seriously.

The Have-Not Provinces

Vigorous resistance to the ACCESS proposals was expressed by a number of people reflecting the views of governments and people in the fiscally weaker provinces. There was strong scepticism about whether these initiatives were genuinely in the interests of the country and whether they could and would be fashioned in such a way as to protect the vital interests of communities in parts of the country dependent on equalization.

If Not ACCESS, or Something Like It, Then What?

After a vigorous and extended discussion in which the apparent inadequacies of the ACCESS approach were explored, a hard question was put. If we take the view that the status quo is unstable, and that the Courchene approach is unworkable or undesirable, then what do we think is a better alternative? Are we implicitly falling back on the necessary reassertion of federal power? Or are there other alternative possibilities? No clear response to this discomfiting challenge emerged at the symposium.

COMMENTS ON THE PAPER ITSELF

A number of the interventions addressed aspects of the paper itself.

Level of Generality. Some questions were raised about how much progress can be made in a complex policy field such as this so long as one stays at this highly general level of analysis. The elements of the social and economic union are many, and they are exceedingly diverse; assessing the adequacy of this line of reasoning may ultimately depend on seeing whether and how it works in a very specific policy and program domain. Tying the argument down tightly to empirical reality may be essential if one is to gain a clear idea of the approach's concrete workability.

Compliance. A fair amount of discussion turned on the question of compliance. Most of the debate was grounded in a common recognition that, to talk at all about a social and economic union, was necessary to raise the question of forms and degrees of compliance with its terms. One participant suggested that we were looking for a middle way between money and the courts as a way of achieving social policy goals. Another noted that the country should be concentrating on standards for assessing well-being, not standards for programs ostensibly delivering well-being. Some participants spoke of the importance of developing "soft compliance," "an ethic of compliance," a culture in which politicians would adhere to generally accepted, common practices because of the expectations of their populations and of their intergovernmental colleagues. Some believed that in a federation, where experimentation and variation (implying something different from compliance) were supposed to be good things, the sheer power of example and information exchange should be sufficient, or close to sufficient. Some took the view that the power of public opinion, nurtured by the communication to citizens of information about the functioning of the system, would ensure respect for national norms and common principles; others believed that this device would prove to be far too feeble. Some participants contended that it was a mistake to look for a single pattern of compliance, and that one should be fashioning forms of compliance appropriate to the specific policy areas under negotiation — mutual recognition, delegation, national standards, soft compliance, etc. A good deal of debate revolved around the question of the continued necessity/inevitability of the federal spending power as the most reliable backstop for the system.

The Distinction Between the Logic of the Social and the Economic Union

One participant made an observation which was noted and commented on by some others, namely, that it was a mistake to assume that we were talking about a single system, at least so far as its architecture and design were concerned. The interests and behaviour of actors in economic life were quite different from the interests and behaviour of actors in social life, and this imposed a different policy logic on governments operating in the two fields. In the market place, competition is central, and governments are therefore concerned that their economic actors operate in a national system that is fair and open; what happens in other jurisdictions is of direct interest to them. In social policy fields, however, the competitive element is less central, and governments are in consequence less immediately concerned with what occurs in other jurisdictions; therefore, norms and principles need to be rooted in feelings of equity and citizenship, not in the equation created by interlocking self-interest.

Lack of Fiscal Detail in the Paper

Several participants remarked on the lack of detail in the paper concerning the possible fiscal arrangements, for example, with respect to the role of equalization under the new regime and its impact on provinces. It was suggested that the lack of detail may have created more, and more varied, opposition than there needed to be, because people were having to fill in the blanks as best they could by themselves.

Impact of Proposed Regime on Democratic Government

The paper was criticized for its heavy reliance on intergovernmental relations, and the impact its proposals would have on democratic government. It was argued that the ACCESS approach would likely erode legislative politics; accelerate the decline of political parties and principles of political accountability; reinforce the territorial foundations of Canadian political life; and foster a retreat from populism. In general, it would involve a retreat from democratic government in favour of a managerial model of government. In addition, it would make more difficult the achievement of intrastate federalism reforms.

This view was not universally accepted. Some believed that this was an excessively critical burden to lay at the door of one proposal which, after all, was consistent in many ways with the way the country has done much of its fiscal and federal business. It was noted that a slightly different proposal could have begun to integrate the social and economic union approach with the principle of intrastate federalism reforms. One participant exclaimed that we accept the obligations of international treaties, financial markets and the Charter without charging that they are anti-democratic; why can't we accept federal-provincial relations in the same spirit? Why are agreements by 11 first ministers undemocratic?

Some discussion ensued about the possibility of designing into the reform model a robust element of transparency as a way of countering these concerns.

Getting There

With respect to the "implementability" of the proposals, a mixture of hope and scepticism was expressed. Implicitly, it seemed that the interim model attracted greater support on the grounds that it was more realistic and do-able. This feeling seemed to be linked to the interest that was expressed from several quarters in the promising work being done by the Ministerial Council on Social Policy Reform; this approach appeared to several participants to hold out real promise and to be parallel in many respects to the thinking of Tom Courchene's interim model.

WHAT WAS NOT COVERED IN THE DISCUSSION?

The symposium covered a lot of ground, but a number of possible candidates for discussion were not in the event examined.

Detailed Design Questions. Relatively little time was spent examining in detail the architecture and engineering principles of the two models and assessing the workability of specific elements. There was more interest in assessing the broad nature and impact of the Courchene proposals.

Weighing the Two Models Against One Another. Participants were not by and large inclined to evaluate the two models vis-à-vis one another, to consider the relative advisability, workability, and impact of the interim and full ACCESS proposals. Much of the discussion was grounded in the implicit assumption that both models exhibited a similar approach and moved in a consistent direction, and debate revolved around the impact, advisability, and consequences of that approach and direction.

Other Initiatives. There was little opportunity to discuss other initiatives, such as the *Report to Premiers* of the Ministerial Council on Social Policy Reform and Renewal or the work of the CPRN, although the chairman of the symposium, Keith Banting, had explicitly invited such discussion. While participants frequently referred to the Ministerial Council report, it appeared that there was a desire to concentrate at this colloquium on taking stock of the ACCESS approach and the central issues that were raised by it.

The Constitution. Towards the end of the meeting, one participant's pleasantly surprised remark that the symposium had spent the whole day discussing the reform of federalism and not the amendment of the constitution was greeted with nodding heads and palpable satisfaction by most others present.

CONCLUSION

Several observations might be offered by way of conclusion.

As was remarked half-way through the discussion: "ACCESS is a marvellous document, because everyone is able to read something different in it." Indeed, one of the striking features of the discussion was just that; in many cases, people understood the paper to be saying contradictory things.

There appeared to be general agreement that the paper was serving a very useful purpose in crystallizing debate around some central policy issues confronting the Canadian federation.

The symposium moved during the course of the day from criticism to reconciliation — criticism of the gaps and weaknesses people perceived in the ACCESS paper, to emergent agreement concerning the need and opportunity to address the issues Tom's paper was confronting and the utility of the paper in helping all the participants to do so.

There was a strong shared conviction that the system in its current shape was unstable and that significant reform was needed. It would take another conference, however, to reach general agreement on just what that reform should be.

Part Two

ESSAYS

ONE

Canada Needs a Political and Cultural as well as a Social and Economic Covenant

André Burelle

Any assessment of Tom Courchene's paper is bound to be influenced by the personal bias of the assessor. I might as well confess mine right from the start. As Peter Leslie reminded me, I was the first public servant to propose in Ottawa, back in the 1980s, a partnership approach to the management of the interdependence between the two orders of government of our federation. Inspired by Jean Monnet's philosophy, I had coined the expression "gestion fédératrice," translated as "federative management," to describe a concept that gave birth, in 1991, to the proposal of a Pact on the Canadian Social and Economic Union by the research group I was then supervising in our Federal-Provincial Office in Montreal.

I have, since then, recast and explained more fully that proposal in my book *Le mal canadien*. And as the lonely federalist father of that child, published six months before the last referendum in Quebec, allow me to thank all who signed the Manifesto of the Group of 22, for the much needed endorsement of the ideas similar to those put forward in my book. Allow me also to thank Tom Courchene for the new life he has given to those ideas in his own ACCESS proposal.

Having said this, I should rejoice for such a breakthrough in English Canada, but much to my regret, I have to admit that I felt somewhat short-changed after reading Tom's paper. Let me explain why.

First, I find ACCESS extremely insightful in its analysis of the global techno-economic forces that are reshaping Canada but almost blind to the present political dynamics of the country.

As you may remember, during a similar session organized by this Institute in the aftermath of the disastrous referendum of October 1995, I was asked to answer the tough question: "What can we do to bring Quebec back into the fold?" I submitted, then, that the only way this could be accomplished was by putting to Quebec a global proposal to rebalance the Canadian federation that would be both acceptable to a clear majority of Quebecers and viable for the country as a whole. This meant, and still means, that such a proposal had to take into account the sad fact that ever since the collapse of the Meech Lake Accord, Canada has been experiencing not one but two simultaneous "meta-crises." For both what I called the "founding tenet" and the "modern tenet" of the Canadian social and political contract — that is, our initial refusal of the melting-pot approach and our postwar search for equal opportunity among citizens and regions — have been brought into question by:

1. our incapacity, as illustrated by the Meech Lake failure, to combine the individualistic liberalism of the Charter of 1982, as defended by former Prime Minister Trudeau and others, with the collective right to cultural distinctiveness of Quebec which was at the heart of the confederation pact of 1867; and

2. our incapacity, as illustrated by the Axworthy reform failure and the unilateral cuts imposed on provinces by the 1995 federal budget, to consolidate, on a partnership basis, the generous pan-Canadian economic and social programs that are now threatened by the federal debt overload and by the pressures of free trade and the "survival of the fittest" ideology of neoliberals.

Moreover, these two crises are clearly interlinked since our Canadian social net was built, to a large extent, thanks to Ottawa's spending power in areas of exclusive provincial jurisdiction, assigned to Quebec by the constitution to exercise its right to cultural distinctiveness and to all provinces to exercise their right to local self-government. That is why I reached the conclusion several years ago that, in order to solve these two inextricably interlinked crises, one needed to rebalance our federation on the basis of the following equation:

• on the one hand, the right to cultural distinctiveness of Quebec and the Aboriginal Peoples *and* the right of all provinces to local autonomy, with the effective decentralization of powers and responsibilities needed to exercise those rights;

• on the other hand, the obligation of all partners of our federation to decide jointly through a transparent and responsible Council of First Ministers, as they do in the European Union, the common objectives and common constraints they must abide by in the exercise of their respective sovereign powers. They must do this in order to: (i) ensure free movement of goods, services, capital, and persons throughout the Canadian economic union; (ii) guarantee basic social services to all citizens of the country; (iii) harmonize the fiscal and budgetary policies and coordinate the exercise of the sovereign powers of both orders of government; and (iv) permit the country to speak with one voice in a globalized world where the federal government is asked more and more often to sign international treaties in fields of exclusive provincial jurisdiction.

In simple terms, what I proposed in my presentation of last December was a bold but fair "win-win" logic of negotiation: *"Meech plus" and an administrative pact signed by all the partners of the federation to strengthen and modernize the Canadian Social and Economic Union.*

As one can see, in such a perspective, the main purpose of a Pact on the Canadian Social and Economic union was political and cultural, as much as it was social and economic: namely, to move away from nation-building based on the federal spending power at a time when Ottawa could no longer afford to spend, and to consolidate our economic and social union on a partnership basis, in full respect of provincial powers and in full compliance with the "refusal of the melting pot approach" that was at the heart of the Canadian social and political contract of 1867. And as a side benefit, such a pact was intended to provide our federation with the kind of effective and transparent coordinating instrument it needs to tackle the global problems of our time.

Given the fact that we almost lost the last Quebec referendum, I feel strongly that one cannot choose only the social and economic side of that proposal and ignore its cultural and political side without sacrificing the feasibility of the whole reform. In other words, taken out of a win-win logic of negotiation, Tom's proposal is bound to be seen by a majority of Quebecers as a one-sided response of the Rest of Canada (ROC), deprived of any serious consideration for Quebec's need for recognition and cultural security.

My second point is that even if it was part of a win-win package, Tom's proposal would have to be reworked to be acceptable to a majority of Quebecers, because it is long on social rights and short on the intergovernmental dynamics and institutions that would be required to deliver on those rights in full respect of our Canadian political contract. In fact, Tom's convention could easily, though mistakenly, be read in Quebec as a "chartist" rather than a "partnership" proposal to preserve and strengthen Canada's social and economic union. When Tom writes, for instance, that his "convention on the socio-economic union, while of necessity an agreement among governments, is first and foremost about the rights and privileges of citizens, consumers, labour and enterprise on the socioeconomic front"; and when he adds that his convention " is a set of social and economic rights of citizens and private sector agents" that will result in a transfer of sovereignty "to individual Canadians," he may speak a language that will please a certain clientele in the ROC, but he is using words that painfully remind Quebecers of Trudeau's "people package" of 1982.

For my part, I feel that this kind of distrustful reading is bound to happen in Quebec because, in the description he gives of both his interim and his full ACCESS model, Tom remains vague on the institutional instruments and the decision-making process they would need to work in a true partnership mode. I also believe that even his less ambitious interim model will be resisted in Ottawa and will not be put in place by "the stroke of a pen." Having worked for so many years at the federal level, I think that "unitarian" nation-building through spending power is so embedded in the culture of our federal leaders in Ottawa, that it would take almost a "democratic coup d'état" by the provinces to provoke the change of mentality needed to implement even Tom's minimalist model. When federal ministers and public servants talk about subsidiarity, they do not see it as a bottom-up process but as a top-down exercise through which our senior "national" government "devolves" or "delegates" powers to junior "provincial" governments. They never mention the federal principle of non-subordination, and it never comes to their mind that the central government cannot delegate or devolve powers that already belong to the provinces by virtue of the constitution.

I think Tom is more to the point when he writes that the federal government is actually presuming that "the provinces will never get their act together" and that citizens' support will go to "a strong central role, even a unilateral role" for Ottawa in "monitoring and policing the socio-economic union." In fact, if provinces do not get their act together, I submit that they could very well build a winning platform for the Chrétien government as the "left-wing"saviour of our "national social programs" jeopardized by "right-wing" provinces.

I also believe that Ottawa will resist even more Tom's full-ACCESS model and will attack it, partly with good reason, as relying too much on interprovincialism. Tom may be right in thinking that interprovincialism could be the first step in bringing provinces "to shoulder enhanced 'pan-Canadian' responsibilities commensurate with their increased powers," but nobody can deny that, in our day and age, managing the interdependence between governments in a federation is much more than managing interprovincial relations. The simple truth is that Canada is already facing, and will face even more often tomorrow, global problems that fall neither under exclusive provincial jurisdiction nor under exclusive federal jurisdiction. Those problems can only be solved by both orders of government working together and exercising in a complementary way their respective sovereign powers. And to ensure that kind of coordination, what is needed is a transparent and efficient tool to manage, on a partnership basis, the interface between the two orders of government of the Canadian federation. The same applies to the ever-increasing number of international treaties Ottawa has to negotiate and promises to implement in fields of exclusive provincial jurisdiction. Even our Canadian social union calls, one could argue, for more than a simple interprovincial approach, since the 1982 *Constitution Act* says explicitly that "Parliament and the legislatures, together with the government of Canada and the provincial governments, are committed" to equal opportunity for citizens and regions.

But all is not lost, as we found out in Montreal. With a Council of First Ministers able to practice European-style co-decision, according to decision rules unanimously agreed upon by all players, Canada could manage both its interprovincial and federal-provincial relations. Such a council would operate as an interprovincial body on occasions when the provinces have the authority to vote in fields of exclusive provincial jurisdiction. It would operate as a federal-provincial body in all cases where the federal government as well as the provinces are entitled to vote.

Moreover, and this is central to the concept of "federative management" of the interface between both orders of government:

- any matter requiring unanimity would be decided in a confederative mode, since all partners would exercise a veto and thus retain full control of the sovereign powers assigned to them by the constitution; and

- any matter that would only require a weighted or simple majority would be decided in a federal mode, since all partners would agree to submit the exercise of their sovereign powers to the will of the majority.

Let me simply conclude my admittedly biased assessment of ACCESS by the following remarks. Tom's paper can be looked at in a scholarly and purely speculative perspective. Despite my philosophical background, I resisted that temptation and chose to assess it from a political and practical point of view, because what Canada needs urgently, in the aftermath of the 1995 referendum, is a set of new *workable* ideas. And despite my pessimistic comments, I still believe that Tom's ideas could become workable if they were amended and made part of a larger win-win solution to our collective problems.

For what Canada needs, in my mind, is a political and cultural as well as a social and economic covenant. One that would not only save our social and economic union, but that would, at the same time, strengthen our will to live together and give this country the spirit uplift, "le supplément d'âme," it needs to overcome the "need for recognition crisis" that has been poisoning the atmosphere between Quebec and the ROC ever since patriation and the collapse of the Meech Lake Accord.

TWO

The Enforcement of Intergovernmental Accords

Katherine Swinton

INTRODUCTION

Tom Courchene's ACCESS paper is generating a much-needed discussion about the management of the Canadian federal system. While I sympathize with the need for a new approach, my comments address three main points with respect to the ACCESS proposal: one deals with its scope; a second deals with the binding nature of intergovernmental agreements and undertakings; and the third, and most important, deals with the design of enforcement mechanisms in intergovernmental relations.

THE SCOPE OF THE ACCESS PROJECT

At the level of the "full model," the ACCESS document proposes a massive undertaking for the rearrangement of the federal system, incorporating many features of the 1992 Charlottetown Accord with respect to the distribution of powers, and more. The proposal includes a greater provincial role in creating and enforcing national standards for social policy; improved coordination between provinces and the federal government in areas such as macroeconomic policy and treaty making, a new section 121 of the constitution dealing with mobility in the economic union, mutual recognition of occupational qualifications — and the list continues.

All of this is to be brought within one convention, with subaccords. This looks like mega-constitutional reform in a new guise; it certainly would require an ambitious exercise of what Stefan Dupré once called "summit federalism" (Dupré 1985, p. 1) The lack of success at large-scale reform through summitry in the last few years makes me doubt that we would be any more successful in negotiating a broad umbrella convention of the sort contemplated here, even were Quebec willing to participate.

Therefore, rather than think about the project of reshaping intergovernmental relations as focused on the production of one accord, it is more realistic to think about incremental changes, often brought about through "functional federalism" in various policy areas. This would continue the trend already set in place by the Internal Trade Agreement in 1994 or the more recent report of the provincial ministerial council on social policy reform and renewal. These and other developments may ultimately result in a number of accords. Some might set fairly precise standards of conduct; for example, the right to portability in health care or the prohibition of residency requirements for the receipt of social assistance, to use two examples already conditions for receipt of federal funds under the Canada Health and Social Transfer (CHST). But other accords are likely to be more process-oriented, committing governments to further action on a problem, for example, setting occupational standards. With respect to the latter issue, while Courchene sees this as an easy area for agreement, he ignores the fact that there can be legitimate debate about the minimum qualifications necessary for competence and public safety, so that even mutual recognition may not be readily achieved.

Together, these efforts may someday bring us closer to the full ACCESS model. Most importantly, in the process of their development, we will experiment with new institutions for enforcement and dispute resolution in the Canadian federal system.

MAKING INTERGOVERNMENTAL AGREEMENTS BINDING

Courchene's paper is concerned about the inability of our constitutional framework to bind governments, federal or provincial, to agreements should they change their minds at some point, or refuse to comply with obligations when told they are in violation. He is correct in noting that there are obstacles within the Canadian constitutional framework to making these agreements binding, which suggests the need for a provision like section 126A of the Charlottetown Accord, which would have created a process to make agreements legally binding for up to five years. Intergovernmental agreements, like treaties at the international level, are executive acts. Therefore, they cannot change existing laws without some type of implementing legislation. They can, of course, bind the signatory government where they are contractual in nature, although governments can legislate to override contracts, subject to the limits on provincial jurisdiction to avoid contractual obligations with an extraterritorial reach (as Newfoundland has found in relation to its contract with Hydro-Québec in *Upper Churchill Falls*[1]).

As the *CAP Reference* in the Supreme Court of Canada emphasized, parliamentary supremacy is a fundamental principle of our constitutional system, which is not tempered by executive federalism.[2] Therefore, the federal Parliament was able unilaterally to enact legislation changing its financial obligations under the Canada Assistance Plan — both because the terms of its funding obligations were, by statute, subject to variation by legislation, and because parliamentary supremacy prevents one parliament from binding another, in legislation or in an agreement with the provinces. Therefore, parliaments can override agreements, and repeal or change implementing legislation.

There may be one brake on parliamentary supremacy through the device of manner and form legislation, mentioned in ACCESS. While one parliament cannot bind its successors in terms of the substance of legislation, it may be able to enact procedural devices to constrain the legislative process, for example, through specifying a special majority to change a particular law or imposing a referendum requirement. In Canada, manner and form legislation has received little attention, but, with virtually no discussion, courts have accepted the primacy of human rights codes and language guarantees over other legislation, giving them special status. This does not give these laws protection from repeal, but it does allow them to override other statutes, even those enacted after the law accorded primacy.

Could one design the ACCESS convention as manner and form legislation? Courchene seems to want to do this — not just to give primacy to its content, but also to protect it from repeal without special procedures. The latter seems a doubtful course, given the ambitious range of topics that Courchene seeks to include; for example, keeping the federal government from spending in certain areas, transfer of tax points, and economic union guarantees. Making it very difficult to change these obligations would look like an attempt to tie the hands of future governments without a constitutional amendment.

However, it could be feasible to try to give primacy to some elements of the convention that are susceptible to enforcement through adjudication. For example, if governments agreed on a charter of the social and economic union, with broad statements of rights (like the conditions of the *Canada Health Act,* or the proposed section 121, or perhaps a social charter somewhat akin to that in the Charlottetown Accord), courts might see this as analogous to human rights codes and interpret other laws in light of these guarantees; for example, striking down regulations permitting residency requirements for health or social assistance as illegal. However, the likelihood of finding political, and even widespread popular support for such legislation is close to zero, since it contemplates adjudication by courts or perhaps another body to determine highly charged political issues.

DESIGNING ENFORCEMENT MECHANISMS

Should we despair, if we cannot ensure that governments will always be legally bound by agreements? Elsewhere I have suggested that we should not, recognizing that there are ways to enforce intergovernmental obligations (Swinton 1995, p. 196). In some cases, we can resort to existing mechanisms, such as the spending power with respect to the CHST conditions (although for reasons of legitimacy, with the declining federal financial contribution to health and social assistance, a provincial role in determining non-compliance with the conditions seems warranted). Even where that "incentive" is not available, the lack of binding agreements does not mean the end of the rule of law, where there are political forces creating an ethic of compliance; for example, where there is popular support for compliance, perhaps to avoid sanctions against the province, as under the Internal Trade Agreement.

In the spirit of incrementalism mentioned earlier, I suggest that we need to be sensitive to the range of enforcement mechanisms for intergovernmental agreements and to the fact that the utility of each mechanism varies with the type of governmental obligation. Therefore, I do not contemplate one model applicable to one umbrella convention, but a range of alternatives tailored to the policy area and the obligations assumed.

In some areas, intergovernmental agreement may lead to delegation of duties to an administrative body or another government. That seems to be one likely avenue for creating a national securities commission, which would then be empowered to develop a national securities policy. This is a longstanding tool in our federal system, as seen, for example, in operation of agricultural products marketing boards.

In other areas, governments may commit to certain standards, some of which are easy to apply, and some which are not because of their open-ended nature. Depending on the kind of obligation, governments are likely to consider different types of enforcement mechanisms. For example, mutual recognition agreements respecting occupational qualifications from other Canadian jurisdictions are easy to apply. They could be enforced effectively through implementing legislation in each jurisdiction and court oversight, launched by individual litigants or governments.

Other obligations are more difficult to agree upon, such as the meaning of accessibility or what constitute user fees under the *Canada Health Act*, or the concept of a trade barrier in many areas. Here, the emphasis may best be put on designing standards where agreement can be reached but agreeing to *processes* for harmonization and the development of standards over time in more complex areas. That is the model of the Internal Trade Agreement and there is much to be said for it.

In terms of enforcement, an adjudicative mechanism open to both governments and citizens may be suitable where standards are prescribed; for example, in dealing with non-discrimination in government procurement. It is then important to ask whether there is a need for special expertise that would best be found in a specialized adjudicative body, rather than the superior courts.

Where processes are agreed upon, government reporting on progress and compliance, with monitoring by some publicly accountable process, might be more realistic and effective than adjudication. This is the model of international human rights conventions, especially in respect of the implementation of social and economic rights. Often, there is no formal sanction associated with a finding of deficiencies, but the associated publicity is designed to put pressures on governments to take appropriate action to comply.

CONCLUSION

Tom Courchene is right to urge Canadians to think about the operation of the social and economic union, with careful attention to the role of intergovernmental relations. While the hope may be that one day we will have broad agreement on framework principles for intergovernmental relations, we should not lose sight of the benefits of incrementalism and functional federalism, which will allow us to make progress in the design of decision-making and enforcement mechanisms suited to particular policy areas, while exploring the many other important issues associated with the ACCESS proposal, including democratic and distributional concerns, discussed elsewhere in this volume.

NOTES

1. *Churchill Falls(Labrador) Corp.* v. *A.G. Nfld.* (1984), 8 D.L.R.(4th) 1 (S.C.C.).
2. *Reference re: Canada Assistance Plan (B.C.)* (1991), 83 D.L.R.(4th) 297.

REFERENCES

Dupré, J.S. (1985), "Reflections on the Workability of Executive Federalism" in *Intergovernmental Relations*, ed. R. Simeon (Toronto: University of Toronto Press).

Swinton, K. (1995), "Law, Politics, and the Enforcement of the Agreement on Internal Trade," in *Getting There: An Assessment of the Agreement on Internal Trade*, ed. M.J. Trebilcock and D. Schwanen (Toronto: C.D. Howe Institute).

THREE

Is ACCESS Politically Feasible?

Peter Leslie

I agree with Tom Courchene when he writes: "the provinces have to be brought more fully and more formally into the key societal goal of preserving and promoting social Canada," or the Canadian social union. The policies covered by this "key societal goal" include defining and realizing broadly similar social entitlements for all Canadians. This requires the adoption of minimum standards in income security, health care, and postsecondary education, and it requires that adequate labour-market training be widely available in all parts of Canada.

The proposed convention, as the acronym ACCESS indicates, would have both an economic and a social aspect; in fact, Courchene describes these as being closely related. However, in my comments I shall discuss only the social aspect.

The full ACCESS model prescribes that the provinces should not merely be *involved* in setting and implementing common standards in health, social services, and education; they should have exclusive control of such policies. Indeed, as regards program design, administration, and finance the provinces would be fully in charge of almost all aspects of social policy and "human capital policy" including most payments or expenditures from a jointly managed unemployment insurance fund. It would appear that Ottawa would retain responsibility only for certain parts of the income security/support system (public pensions and tax credits). In all other respects, minimum national standards in social policy would be established by interprovincial agreement, supported by federal equalization payments. The federal government would give up most of the social policy role it had earlier built for itself, mainly between 1942 and 1971. In practice, the commitment imposed upon Parliament and the provincial legislatures under the 1982 *Constitution Act*, to provide "essential public services of reasonable quality to all Canadians" would be held to apply almost exclusively to the legislatures. The remaining two commitments under section 36 (1) of this Act would presumably be federal-provincial rather than interprovincial: Parliament would undoubtedly have a significant role in "promoting equal opportunities for the well-being of all Canadians" through employment-creating activities or strategies, and arguably would have the main responsibility for "furthering economic development to reduce disparity in opportunities." In short, Ottawa's role in the economy might be dominant, but in social policy, its role would be limited to (i) making non-discretionary income support payments to certain classes of persons, and (ii) making equalization payments to the have-not provinces.

My comments focus on the political feasibility of the full ACCESS model. Four questions arise:

1. What might induce provincial governments to establish common or similar standards, and to uphold them over time?

2. What changes in the fiscal arrangements would be needed to sustain common or similar standards across Canada?

3. What might induce the federal government to withdraw from all aspects of health, social services, and education; to pass much of the responsibility for unemployment insurance to the provinces; and to transfer tax points instead of cash to the provinces?

4. Is asymmetry workable — does the ACCESS model require that all provinces commit themselves to minimum national standards, or could some provinces (notably, one assumes, Quebec) stay out?

PROVINCIALLY-SET STANDARDS?

The ACCESS model calls for commitment by all provinces to common minimum standards in social policy. Is this really in the cards?

The question may be addressed by considering two phases: (i) a *launch* phase during which provincial governments — and, following their lead, the legislatures — would decide whether or not to "sign on" to a convention that one province, or a group of provinces, had put forward and (ii) an *implementation* or *compliance* phase of indefinite duration,[1] during which successive provincial governments were required to fund and administer policies that would fulfil the initial commitment, assuming that it had been made. Both phases would appear, at least to me, to raise serious practical difficulties.

Assuming the commitments written into a proposed convention were understood to be real and substantial, the launch phase would be akin — although Courchene's case presumes otherwise — to making a constitutional amendment. The similarities derive from the following facts: the convention would have no termination date; as a practical matter it would have to be approved by all or most provinces[2] within a set period of time, during which almost certainly one or more provinces would experience a turnover in governing party; it would bind future governments and legislatures; and its precise implications for each of the provinces, in terms of program design and required expenditure, would be unclear (that is, they would be subject to interpretation by some agency outside the province, or certainly outside the control of the provincial government). Each of these factors would make provincial governments reluctant to sign a convention that had any substance to it. Nonetheless it is imaginable that public pressure in favour of the convention might be considerable, as Courchene suggests it would be, and provincial governments might be forced into "signing on" more or less against their better judgement. Whatever my misgivings, then, for the sake of argument I propose to assume that public pressure — or political momentum from whatever source — will be great enough for the commitment to be made, at least by most provinces. If we do not assume this, then no further questions arise.

Appropriately, Courchene devotes nearly a quarter of his ACCESS paper to the issues of compliance, enforcement, and remedies. In discussing them, I shall limit myself to political rather than to legal aspects — appropriate, perhaps, because for Courchene what is important is to make an interprovincial agreement "binding politically if not constitutionally." He suggests that violation of nationally agreed-upon norms "could involve expulsion from the internal union so that the mobility provisions no longer apply to the residents of the province." There would be a dispute-resolution process that citizens could access (invoke) directly, without having to gain endorsement from a provincial government. However, complaints validated by a screening panel would be taken up by the relevant provincial governments, which would seek a compromise solution. If no compromise were reached, the complaints would be passed on to an arbitral panel analogous to those provided for under the Agreement on Internal Trade or under the NAFTA. The panel could recommend that an offending province rescind "some particular legislative provision;" non-compliance with the recommendation would entail (presumably mandatory) withdrawal from the convention (my summary).

In my view, all this is pure fantasy, based on serious confusion as to what is involved in maintaining common standards in social policy. The source of the confusion is a false analogy between prohibiting discrimination against non-residents, and, within each province, guaranteeing citizen entitlements to public services. In the former class of cases, it may be alleged that a province ("province A") has established barriers to the movement of goods, services, capital, or persons to the supposed benefit of its own residents but to the detriment of residents of other provinces. In such cases it is reasonable to suppose that the governments of these provinces may seek to defend their residents' interests vis-à-vis the government of province A. However, in the second class of cases, the ones pertinent to supporting common minimum standards in social policy, what is at issue is a person's claims against his or her own provincial government. Why then should province B insist that province A should meet its obligations to its own residents? Courchene's answer is that if A lets its standards slip, then B may be forced to lower its standards too;[3] but against this argument is set another, which I think is more powerful: if B were instrumental in seeing that A met its obligations to its own residents, then B too would be liable, a little further down the road, to similar injunctions. As a rule, governments do not like laying themselves open to future claims, perhaps costly ones, imposed upon it by another agent (a province, a court, a secretariat, an arbitral panel). They tend to like escape mechanisms, ones that they can invoke. Courchene's proposal requires them to act in disregard of their own interests, exposing themselves to future expenditure demands which they could not control.

ACCESS AND THE FISCAL ARRANGEMENTS: REDISTRIBUTIVE EFFECTS

An enormous gap in Courchene's presentation of the ACCESS model is that he does not discuss its redistributive consequences. What these are or would be, depends on details that are (quite reasonably) not spelled out in the ACCESS paper, but it is surprising that the issue of redistribution is not flagged as a factor affecting the acceptability of the model, as far as the fiscally weaker provinces are concerned. It is as if no province need fear being placed in a worse financial position than it would be without ACCESS, and as if Ottawa need not fear any impairment of its future fiscal position. These two suppositions simply do not go together; if one holds, the other cannot. In fact it seems that neither holds.

The ACCESS model calls for an end to fiscal transfers to the provinces for social policy, except through equalization. Under ACCESS, the $11 billion floor in cash transfers to the provinces under the Canadian Health and Social Transfer (CHST), due to be reached at the turn of the century, would be converted into tax points; the value of these tax points would grow thereafter, along with the economy (assuming future increases in GDP).

The transfer of tax points is accomplished by cutting federal tax rates, an action that enables the provinces to raise their taxes by a like amount without further burdening the taxpayer. Automatically, under the existing equalization formula, any increase in provincial income tax yields triggers an increase in equalization; thus, with a transfer of tax points, seven provinces would receive augmented equalization payments from the federal treasury, with two results: (i) Ottawa's expenditures under the equalization program would continue to grow indefinitely, as of course would the *revenues foregone* (i.e., the taxes otherwise flowing into the federal treasury); and (ii) three provinces (Ontario, Alberta, and British Columbia, whose revenues are above the equalization threshold) would gain relative to the other seven. Thus, all provinces would gain but unequally so (the seven "have-nots" would receive CHST-replacement income close to the national average but below that of the three richest provinces).

Given the mechanics of converting cash into tax points, the following observations seem apposite:

- If Ottawa is to avoid incurring a net cost even during the first year of the new system, the value of the tax point transfer would have to be less than $11 billion; the cost of associated equalization would have to be subtracted first. However, it is likely that provinces would feel cheated if they received a tax point transfer lower than the announced $11 billion floor for the CHST.

- The only way to avoid redistribution in favour of the wealthier provinces by converting cash (distributed on an equal per capita basis) into tax points, would be to *fully equalize* the tax points. In other words, for these particular provincial revenues, equalization would have to be set at the level of the highest-income province, not at the existing five-province standard. The potential fiscal burden on Ottawa would be high.

- Given the complexity of equalizing the tax point transfer to the level of the highest-income province, and what I presume would be the unacceptability of doing anything less (because of adverse redistributive consequences for the poorer provinces), implementation of the ACCESS model would probably require fundamental redesign of the fiscal arrangements.

INCENTIVES FOR OTTAWA

Courchene argues that fiscal pressure will induce further decentralization of the federation; he suggests that it is simply not realistic to suppose otherwise. Further, if the socio-economic union is secured, the rationale for federal cash transfers to the provinces, as a means of enforcing national standards or policy principles, will disappear. Implicitly: if Ottawa could be sure that the responsibilities it earlier assumed through the spending power will in future be met by the provinces on their own, it would be willing to exit from the social policy field (except for certain income security/support programs). I doubt this.

The first reason for doubt is that the federal government would have to be confident that existing citizen entitlements would be, if anything, strengthened rather than weakened by its full and final withdrawal from the fields of health care, social services, postsecondary education, and workforce training, *and that the public would perceive its withdrawal as having this consequence.* Merely to state this is to demonstrate the unlikelihood of federal withdrawal. Governments do not generally like to admit publicly abandoning popular programs, medicare being the textbook example, even if those programs are costly. Governments have to be seen to be doing things that people want them to do, and it seems quite clearly established that Ottawa's role as guarantor of the social safety net is one of them. In this respect, its role has already been substantially weakened as a result of budget cuts; for this it has been sharply criticized, and it seems doubtful that complete and final withdrawal, with all the symbolism that withdrawal would entail, is politically likely. The basic maxim here, formulated by Vernon Fowke over 40 years ago, is "A government without functions is a government without respect" (Fowke 1978, p. 247). Governments do not like to see their most widely recognized and most popular functions pass on to other jurisdictions.

The attractiveness to Ottawa of accepting ACCESS is, fiscally speaking, nil. In fact it is negative. The whole of Courchene's argument is predicated on the assumption that Ottawa will be unable or unwilling in future to go on paying for the CHST. But he also says that ACCESS would be implemented through a tax point transfer to the provinces, and that the value of the tax points transferred would increase over time. Add to this the probable additional cost of paying extra equalization (depending on the equalization formula employed, and the number of tax points transferred). In the end, Ottawa either gains no fiscal room at all, or (more likely) loses fiscally as well as in terms of voter/citizen support. It is impossible to argue simultaneously that fiscal pressure will drive the federal government from health care and so forth, but also to assume that the provinces will be fully compensated by Ottawa when it cancels the CHST.

ACCESS AND ASYMMETRY

In terms of underlying political dynamics, the presentation of the ACCESS model is weakest in its neglect of any reference to Quebec. Would ACCESS be viable if Quebec did not sign on, or (to generalize) if provincial participation were less than total? For example, could ACCESS be launched if the general formula for constitutional amendment (seven provinces comprising at least half the Canadian population) applied?

Courchene avoids this question by denying that it could actually arise. He alludes to what happened in Australia, where three of six states agreed to mutual recognition of certain classes of economic regulation, after which "citizens of [the three] other states effectively demanded that their own states also sign on." Without pausing to ask whether federalism works any differently in Canada than in Australia, or whether commitment to common standards in social policy has a different dynamic from moves towards the mutual recognition of regulations, Courchene draws the following conclusion:

> Carried over to the Canadian scene, the real challenge becomes one of finding four or five provinces to begin the process of developing principles and legislation for securing the socio-economic union. At this point, the process will develop a dynamic that will virtually ensure that all other provinces will come on board: their citizens will settle for nothing less (Courchene 1996, pp. 37-38).

I do not believe this. Especially, I do not believe that Quebec would enter into a permanent commitment to align its social policies with those in the rest of Canada — certainly not under the PQ, and almost as surely not under a Liberal government in Quebec City.[4] Quebec did not participate in the interprovincial ministerial council that proposed, in December 1995, "a new and genuine partnership between federal and provincial/territorial governments" in social policy.[5] Moreover, prior to the Annual Premiers' Conference in August 1996 Premier Bouchard warned his fellow premiers against taking a national approach in fields of provincial jurisdiction. At that conference, while Ontario and Alberta liked the ACCESS proposal, the others (excluding Quebec) sought federal-provincial partnership, not a purely interprovincial agreement.

Given such attitudes, it is important to ask whether ACCESS, or indeed a different federal-provincial model, could be put into place without ten-province participation. In my comments on this, I shall limit myself to the possibility of reshaping the Canadian social union without formal participation by Quebec. (By stressing *formal* participation, I leave open the possibility that Quebec could choose not to enter into binding commitments, but might choose to align its policies with those extant in the rest of Canada.)

I could imagine a Canadian social union, supported by a convention along the lines that Courchene has proposed, if it had a financial component that the ACCESS model does not provide for. Rather than transferring tax points to the provinces, which in practice is an irrevocable step, Ottawa could commit a certain number of tax points to a jointly managed (federal-provincial) Canadian social fund. Personally, I would want equalization as well as a variety of social programs to be financed from the fund, in which case quite a few tax points would have to be allocated to it. Thus, replacement of the CHST would be part of a far larger initiative for joint federal-provincial management of the Canadian social union.

Probably the way to launch the fund, and to make a convention on the Canadian social union operational, would be to use the device of *tax abatements*: taxpayers from provinces that adhered to the convention would deduct a certain percentage of the tax otherwise payable to the federal treasury, the money being sent instead to the fund. The overall tax bill would be unaffected, but this scheme would publicize the fact that a portion of the taxes paid were being directed to some combination of income security, health care, and other social purposes, to be spent in accordance with the principles set out in the convention. Administration could be federal-provincial or interprovincial, but it would not be within the power of Parliament or any federal minister to enforce or apply the convention. This scheme would be similar to the *interim* ACCESS model, except that it would not be a temporary improvisation. In fact, it would be in keeping with the December 1995 recommendations of the Ministerial Council on Social Policy Reform and Renewal. If the fund were not operating according to Parliament's satisfaction — say, if Parliament felt the convention was not being applied in good faith, then it would have the power — say, after giving three years' notice, or upon confirmation by a subsequent Parliament (i.e., after a federal election) — to redirect the tax abatements back into the federal treasury. Such a rule, given effect through "manner and form" legislation, (Courchene 1996, p. 26) would imbue these arrangements with a substantial degree of predictability and political protection.

The fund would not be operational, nor would the tax abatements apply, until a specified number of provinces had signed onto the convention. It could also be specified that if the number of provinces ever fell below the threshold, as a result of provincial withdrawals, the whole scheme would be dissolved. In effect, Ottawa would be left to decide when the new system was financially viable. For example, it could be specified that all provinces *not* receiving equalization would have to join and to remain within it; in this way, Ontario, Alberta, and British Columbia would all exercise a veto, but that means each would bear the opprobrium if a joint federal-provincial Canadian social union did not get going, or were later dismantled.

With such a rule, or probably with a rule of "two-thirds of the provinces, with at least two-thirds of the population," the scheme would be financially viable without Quebec's participation. In that case, Ottawa would presumably let Quebec taxpayers "abate" their federal taxes by the value of the social union tax points. Their taxes would be lower than in other provinces, but Quebec, unlike other provinces, would be solely responsible for financing its social programs (without equalization). Different people would have different recommendations and predictions on what would happen, but my own predictions and opinions are: (i) Quebecers, faced with a decision to be "in or out" of the Canadian social union (especially if the fund covered equalization and various income security programs) would choose to stay in; (ii) the likelihood of this would be increased if the question were put to Quebecers by referendum rather than being left to the National Assembly; (iii) if I am wrong on this, and Quebec stayed outside the Canadian social union, I think that Quebec would still align its policies, in practice, with those of the union, and that portability of entitlements would be negotiated; and (iv) if this too is wrong, non-alignment on social policy is better for the rest of us than independence, which I believe would destroy the economic union as well as the social union, leading to fissure of the rest of Canada.

CONCLUSION

The full ACCESS model is, in my opinion, deeply flawed, partly because I cannot imagine the political conditions under which it could be accepted and made to work. I am much more attracted to Courchene's interim model, which is akin to the proposals of the Ministerial Council on Social Policy Reform and Renewal (December 1995). What is needed is, first, a positive federal response to those proposals, and second, a mechanism to implement them. An ACCESS-type convention is a necessary component of a new federal-provincial sharing of responsibilities, though I would, by preference, split it in two. I would convert the Agreement on Internal Trade into a broader convention on the economic union, and I would work for the negotiation of a separate federal-provincial convention on the Canadian social union. The social union would be supported and made operational by the establishment of a Canadian social fund into which earmarked tax revenues would be channelled. If the social union did not work, the tax points would revert to the federal treasury. Quebec could be in or out, as its voters decided.

NOTES

1. It is not specified by Courchene that the convention would be of indefinite duration, but the whole scheme would make no sense if it were time-limited.
2. The issue of asymmetry will be discussed below.
3. I have revised this part of my comments after their oral presentation, to take account of Courchene's responses during the discussion at the roundtable. What is puzzling about his response is that on the one hand he presumes that public opinion will demand that provinces adopt common standards; but on the other hand he also presumes that if one province (province A) gets away with reneging on its commitments in any given area, public support for maintaining standards will wither in the other provinces, one after the other – and that fear of this will lead the other provinces to insist that province A offer the services it has promised to do.
4. This statement may be regarded as unduly negative, in light of a speech by Jean-Marc Fournier, the Quebec Liberal Party's spokesman on Canadian intergovernmental affairs, in August 1996. Mr. Fournier proposed an "interprovincial decision-making process" in which common decisions might be made by provincial governments on subjects lying within provincial jurisdiction. Unanimity would not be required, suggested Mr. Fournier, in all cases. However, he also said that unanimous consent would undoubtedly be required for the most sensitive issues, and that a rule of less-than-

unanimity might be tried for a five-year period only (suggesting no permanent commitment to decisions made during that time). The whole thrust of his presentation was apparently on economic union issues, for example, interprovincial agreements relating to the construction industry; nowhere was there any reference to common or minimum standards in social policy. ("Interprovincialism, a New Canadian Dynamic," unpublished text of speech, August 1996).

5. Ministerial Council on Social Policy Reform and Renewal, *Report to Premiers*, December 1995, p. 1.

REFERENCES

Courchene, T.J. (1996), *ACCESS: A Convention on the Canadsan Economic and Social Systems*, Working Paper (Toronto: Ministry of Intergovernmental Affairs).

Fowke, V.C. (1978), "The National Policy — Old and New," [1952], in *Approaches to Canadian Economic History*, ed. W.T. Easterbrook and M.H. Watkins (Toronto: Macmillan).

FOUR

Reimagining Canada: Decentralized Federalism by Fate or Will?

David Milne

Let me begin my commentary on Thomas Courchene's intriguing essay, ACCESS, by frankly expressing my admiration for the daring and imagination that he has brought to our thinking on this difficult and intractable subject. There is probably no other academic in the country who would so boldly let his mind take free flight in this way, who would purport to see and predict historical forces and patterns, and who would seek to stir provincial political actors to decisive, strategic action.

Courchene's sketch of our current condition identifies a variety of historical forces that are inexorably driving us towards decentralization. Globalization and the information revolution, he argues, push all developed countries in this direction, though Canada is even more exposed to decentralization because of our growing dependence on international trade, our increasingly north-south regional trading system, and our debt and deficit crisis. All of this, in turn, leads "social policy [to undergo] substantial, indeed unprecedented decentralization" (Courchene 1996, p. 2). It is an easy leap from here to argue that we have "no choice" but to bring provinces much more fully and formally into decisive leadership positions over the Canadian social and economic union. The remainder of the paper is devoted to fleshing out two models of doing that, one frankly advanced as merely a transitional system, and the other a full ACCESS model of interprovincial control and responsibility for the Canadian social and economic union.

We begin our commentary by looking at the framework assumptions of Courchene's paper, for it is here where the reader encounters so many strands of apparent inevitability and fate in his argument. Globalization, fiscal overhang, and other forces, it is said, are inexorably driving us toward "unprecedented decentralization," leaving us "no status quo" and "no choice" but to accept this new evolutionary decentralizing reality. Much of this argument about the weakening if not demise of the nation state harkens back to old integrationist arguments that are being increasingly challenged in Europe as elsewhere. Is there really any reason to suppose that the dynamics and effects of globalization are so simple and uni-directional? And if this is true — if the political future is not really foreordained — there will continue to be plenty of room for people to assert their ideological preferences and to draw different conclusions about the long-term effects of such forces. Certainly, this kind of debate among federalism analysts is already underway without any definitive conclusions. In my view, not only is it quite possible that global forces may produce complex effects pointing *simultaneously* in centralizing and decentralizing directions, but the crucial role of history and political culture will undoubtedly have much to say about how different peoples come to terms with global forces.

The same caution might appear to be appropriate in considering the fiscal premises of Courchene's argument. Here, too, the paper's apparent assumption of rapid and irreversible federal decline arising from the fiscal overhang may no longer be appropriate. We now know that Ottawa is moving rather rapidly to get its fiscal house in order; a balanced budget is within sight, while prospects are encouraging for economic growth with low inflation and with interest rates at their lowest level in forty years. Economists like John MacCallum are already arguing that we have in these conditions the makings of a monumental fiscal turnaround unthinkable for decades — a future where the debt-to-GDP ratio will fall steadily even if Ottawa does little more than hold the budget in balance. If so, these are scarcely conditions that will force Ottawa out of the game.

Although Courchene tries on the one hand to paint a future of irresistible decentralization, at other points in his analysis it is obvious that such a result is anything but foreordained. Despite the assertion that "Ottawa is not really a player in the social policy design and delivery game" and that its old instruments under the spending power for preserving the social union have lost their bite and utility, he is forced to admit that in the current status quo, Ottawa is still very much a player, and its spending power methods still operative. Indeed, Courchene is forced to include Ottawa and rely upon precisely these instruments in his own transitional model, albeit with provinces having more say. He is also forced to recognize that citizens, particularly outside Quebec, do not look to the provinces for this kind of collective leadership on behalf of the social and economic union, nor do they seriously expect that provinces can deliver it. In fact, his scenario depends upon exhorting the provinces "to assume this larger responsibility for preserving and promoting social Canada," even while acknowledging the difficulty of getting all of the provinces to accept and to enforce such a Convention on the Canadian Social and Economic Systems. In short, ACCESS will not come to Canadians by fate, nor by a national consensus of citizen values, but at best by an act of decisive will by "four or five provinces," aided by an astonishing combination of federal acquiescence and convention "contagion" in the other provinces (ibid., pp. 6-7, 37-38).

What then of the political feasibility of ACCESS? Under what conditions could we go from here to there? Courchene is right, I think, to see that the steps needed to put in place the interim model appear to be straightforward and do-able, although it is questionable whether any Quebec government would participate. After all, this exercise in co-determination would, in effect, legitimize the use of the federal spending power in provincial areas of jurisdiction; this agency would also have even more clout and authority in its interventions into what are supposed to be, after all, autonomous areas of provincial jurisdiction. An interprovincial convention to which Quebec had acceded would certainly find more favour as a monitoring agency; it is worth recalling in this respect the strong preference of former Premier Lévesque in the late 1970s to have an interprovincial agreement guaranteeing minority language rights rather than constitutional entrenchment. But the question of intrusion into Quebec's sovereignty over social policy by a monitoring agency dominated by majority anglophone governments still remains: What could possibly entice Quebecers to grant this kind of intrusion into their own domain? This is especially so in the sensitive field of social policy where the question of Quebec's distinctiveness might be expected to take its own unique form.

The going might be easier with respect to an interprovincial monitoring of the economic union, but here too, there would be considerable disquiet over any proposal to enhance the power of the Supreme Court over Quebec through a strengthened section 121. The same would be true, of course, of many other provinces of all political stripes which have, for the last 20 years or more, had the most serious reservations about any such course of action. Based on that experience, I would see a stronger section 121 as a clear non-starter. Courchene's paper hints at the difficulty in securing a genuine interprovincial consensus over an enforceable convention that could then be sold to the Canadian people. Securing agreement among the provinces under normal circumstances is notoriously slow and difficult, with the final product carrying predictably long lists of exceptions and special protections: witness the AIT. Courchene may be right to think that a smaller number of provincial leaders might make for more effective drafters with the goal of bringing the other provinces onside later. But if so, the composition of such a leadership group would have to be very carefully considered to avoid suspicions that it is neither a "rich provinces' club" nor a right-wing ideological agenda. Even then, the challenge would be quite enormous.

The largest political question mark arises over the federal response to ACCESS. Certainly, short of major disruption to the federal system, the full ACCESS model would appear to leave Ottawa with little incentive to preside over a reduction in its own taxing capacity or its own abdication from a role in the social and economic union. Not only would that mean a repudiation of over a half-century of activity in the field through the spending power but also an eventual retreat from its constitutional responsibility in social policy, including unemployment insurance, old age pensions and contributory pensions. Moreover, would Canadians even countenance federal withdrawal from its role in defending the conditions of the *Canada Health Act*? Certainly, so far no governing national political party appears ready to give up this attractive but cynical political role, despite reduced federal transfers for health. In any event, as Courchene acknowledges, federal withdrawal would be out of the question unless a workable ACCESS were ready to be put in place.

Even the interim ACCESS model might give the federal government some pause. Not only might it further isolate Quebec in the federation, it would also mean ceding the principle that a decision on the disbursement of federal funds could ultimately be directed by provincial governments. That level of co-determination would not be an easy transition for Ottawa to make, although the interim model clearly stands the better chance of seeing the light of day under current circumstances.

Perhaps the greatest irony in this paper's bold defence of decentralized federalism is that it should itself offer so very little real scope and promise for independent action by provincial communities without supervision by a central authority of some kind, whether federal, federal-provincial, or interprovincial. If this is what federalism has come to, perhaps somehow we've lost our way.

REFERENCE

Courchene, T.J. (1996), *ACCESS: A Convention on the Canadian Economic and Social Systems*, Working Paper (Toronto: Ministry of Intergovernmental Relations).

FIVE

Democratic Reservations About the ACCESS Models

Roger Gibbins

Thomas Courchene's ACCESS models provide a badly needed focal point for discussions of decentralization. They also represent an imaginative attempt to address the combined pursuit of greater decentralization and the retention of national standards. However, they would also have the effect of further strengthening the role of intergovernmentalism in the Canadian federal state at the expense of democratic principles. In short, pan-Canadianism pursued through intergovernmentalism is not without its costs. Let me explain by addressing five specific concerns.

A DIMINISHED ROLE FOR LEGISLATIVE POLITICS AND INSTITUTIONS

The ACCESS models would have the effect of shifting decision-making power from legislative assemblies, both federal and provincial, to intergovernmental for a Such a shift, of course, is not new to Canadian politics, for executive federalism has long been a defining characteristic of Canadian political life. Nonetheless, the ACCESS models would further erode the importance of legislative institutions, and the importance of politicians serving in federal and provincial legislatures. Social program decisions directly affecting the lives of Canadians would increasingly be made elsewhere, and it is not clear that legislatures would even retain a significant ratification role.

The concern here reaches beyond the further erosion of legislative institutions, although the troubling nature of that erosion should not be overlooked. It extends to democratic accountability. Simply put, can either the federal or provincial governments be held accountable for collective, intergovernmental agreements over which no one government has any effective control? Or will the buck be passed to intergovernmental fora which are not accountable to any given electorate?

REJECTION OF INTRASTATE REFORM FOR PARLIAMENTARY INSTITUTIONS

Over the past several decades a determined (although quite obviously not compelling) argument has been advanced for the intrastate reform of parliamentary institutions in order to make those institutions more regionally-responsive, and thereby to provide a more legitimate and effective national government. This argument has been associated with the promotion of an elected Senate, a reduction in party discipline and, at times, with electoral reform. All of these measures, however, become less important in the ACCESS models as decision-making power shifts to intergovernmental fora. While the ACCESS models would certainly strengthen the role of provincial governments as regional representatives, they do not provide for any strengthening of the linkage between individual citizens and their national government. In this sense, ACCESS represents the abandonment of intrastate reform in favour of interstate federalism channelled through provincial governments.

It is worth noting in passing that the intrastate reform of parliamentary institutions has been primarily a western Canadian preoccupation, although Atlantic premiers have occasionally waded into the fray. Former Newfoundland Premier Clyde Wells, for example, was an enthusiastic fan of Senate reform. The ACCESS models, however, capture a model of the Canadian federal state that finds many of its intellectual roots in the nationalist movement in Quebec. Therefore the ACCESS models constitute a further rejection of western Canadian reform initiatives.

THE EROSION OF POLITICAL PARTIES

One of the most striking characteristics of executive federalism is the minor role played by partisanship. Party politics are an insignificant factor in interprovincial coalition building, and rarely is the intergovernmental stage used for the pursuit of partisan advantage. Of course, one could argue that the exclusion of opposition parties from intergovernmental fora provides a considerable strategic advantage to incumbent partisan governments, but the fact remains that intergovernmentalism tends to restrict the role of partisanship. The ACCESS models would take us further down this road. Just as legislatures would become less important, so too would political parties, partisan debate, and even elections. While this may strike some people as a strength of the ACCESS models, it does pose a problem for accountable government. For better or for worse, political parties and electoral combat provide the primary mechanisms for democratic accountability. Yet political parties, already under attack by a suspicious and cynical public, would be further weakened by the implementation of the ACCESS models.

THE IMPORTANCE OF TERRITORY

The ACCESS models would reinforce the territorial foundations of Canadian political life. As mentioned above, parties that cut across provincial boundaries are largely taken out of play by intergovernmentalism. So too, although perhaps to a lesser extent, are national interest groups and transboundary social movements. The primary actors in the ACCESS world are provincial governments which, by definition, represent territorially defined political communities. Therefore the ACCESS models may bottle up our political identities even more in provincial and regional communities. When we speak in intergovernmental fora, we speak in territorially-defined voices, as British Columbians and Nova Scotians rather than as women, trade unionists, environmentalists, or neoconservatives. Here again it is worth noting that such a territorial definition of political life is very much in line with nationalist thought in Quebec, but at odds with transprovincial interests and identities in the rest of Canada.

THE RETREAT FROM POPULISM

It was only four years ago that nearly 15,000,000 Canadians took part in the referendum on the Charlottetown Accord. Since then, we have seen a growing emphasis on intergovernmentalism as the vehicle for reforming the Canadian federal system. At the rhetorical level, this is linked to decentralization and the conviction that decentralization brings government "closer to the people." However, intergovernmentalism does not bring government closer to the people. Indeed, it moves government as far from the people as one can get. In this sense, the ACCESS models and their concomitant emphasis on intergovernmentalism are a direct repudiation of the recent populist impulse in Canadian politics. Government is entrusted not to the people but to intergovernmental fora which operate beyond the glare of public exposure, and beyond the immediate pressures of democratic accountability.

In summary, the ACCESS models developed by Courchene would, at least at the margins, reduce the role and effective influence of legislatures, political parties, elections, interest groups, and the public. They would promote government that was less accountable and, in that sense, less democratic.

The problem, it should be stressed, does not lie with decentralization per se, for in many cases decentralized government may indeed be "closer to the people."

Nor should intergovernmentalism be portrayed as a blight on the political landscape, for it is an inevitable and essential component of modern government. The problem stems from the combination of decentralization and intergovernmentalism in the ACCESS models, a combination that moves political decisions out of legislatures and into fora relatively insulated from public pressure, partisan debate, and electoral combat. The solution may lie in Alberta Premier Ralph Klein's hesitation in endorsing the ACCESS model. In effect, Klein has argued that decentralization should mean greater programmatic autonomy for provincial governments, and not the entanglement of provincial governments in intergovernmental fora and agreements. We should, he suggests, trust provincial governments and bite the decentralization bullet.

The drawback of the ACCESS models is that in trying to save national standards and programs from decentralization, they impose a measure of intergovernmentalism that may compromise accountable, democratic government. If adopted, the ACCESS models would leave us with government institutions that were more federal, but perhaps less democratic.

SIX

ACCESS: How Do We Get There from Here?

Gordon Gibson

My topic is about what can realistically be done. This is almost independent of the goal for change — whether one wants a "Courchene Canada" or a "Burelle Canada," the operational question is, "How do you get there from here?" Thus, to me the real question of the day is the process, the machinery.

PROBLEMS

There is the matter of federal cooperation with any structural changes that might be devised. This is particularly true of either of the ACCESS models. In my opinion the transfer of tax points required for the "full" model is just not on. Even the minimal cooperation for the "interim" model — this being cooperation in a joint federal-provincial monitoring and enforcement agency — is most unlikely at the moment.

The second problem is this: existing interprovincial cooperation mechanisms are not adequate to even *administer* a full-blown ACCESS model, let alone negotiate and create it in the first place. So even if Ottawa did cooperate, the provinces are not up to the task at the moment.

The third problem relates to Quebec. That province is still in a "duality" mode, and is not ready for even a European Union (EU)-type body in Canada, were one on offer. The problem is: either the EU model (with Canadian provinces substituted) or ACCESS implies rules made by others impacting on the internal social decisions of Quebec. That province will not accept such a regime as long as it sees Ottawa/rest of Canada (ROC) as a monolithic consortium. The demands of duality will back off (if ever) only after it is clear that other Canadian provinces will act with an attitude of Quebec-type independence from Ottawa and each other. Please note — that day may not be far off. Of particular encouragement is the recent tendency of Ontario to act like a *province*, rather than an Ottawa cheerleader.

The fourth problem is the fact that the underlying goal sets are in considerable conflict. On the surface, such splendid things as equality, mobility, and preservation of language and culture seem common ground, but they are not. Whose equality? Equality of provinces, or persons, or "nations"? Whose mobility? The free marketeer who believes that unequal Unemployment Insurance (UI) entitlements and interprovincial trade and occupational barriers distort the social union, or the social protectionist who believes that local jobs and income assistance entitlements to stay in one's province are really the way to go? And whose "language and culture"? The anglophones of Montreal? The "third order of government"?

The fifth problem is time. We may be short of that commodity, in part because of events in Quebec beyond the control of ROC, and in part because the financial pressures recently driving Ottawa to a certain measure of jurisdictional humility may be easing.

ASSETS OR OPPORTUNITIES

But there are more cheerful observations. The first is this: Canada is working quite well. We do not need a revolution to fix it.

Next, Canada (unlike the EU) has legitimate, democratically based governments at both — indeed *all* — levels. This, along with our quite diverse society, gives us a fair shot at developing a pattern of federalism for the twenty-first century. In particular, we start with a leg up on the issue of the so-called "democratic deficit" of intergovernmental institutions.

Third, we are approaching a modest financial flexibility for governments. Some see this as a danger — i.e., an Ottawa with spare change will seek more power. Others see this as an asset. Restructuring is always easier with the lubrication of cash.

Finally, there is no lack of *ideas* for solving our problems of federalism; they abound. The real lack is in *will* and *machinery*.

SOLUTIONS

The first element of solution is to build on what we have. The advantage of this approach is that it permits a continual learning by experience, and a pace that does not too far outrun our information and wisdom. What we have in this area is the system of First Ministers' Conferences (FMCs) and their sectoral emanations, and Annual Premiers' Conferences (APCs) and associated sectoral satellites.

This whole system, for the moment, is characterized by secrecy of process, and crisis-type activity. The irregular (FMC) or regular (APC) meetings have typically been moderated by "Sherpas" (for the summit), with little continuity or interaction with the ongoing, real world. Latterly, and mostly unnoticed by the press or public, the APC level has acquired a great deal more continuity. The report of the social policy ministers (December 1995) is generally acknowledged as a seminal working document. The August 1996 APC directed extensive ongoing work on this and other files. But the process of secrecy remains.

There is, as well, a *fundamental imbalance* in the FMC-APC nexus. The FMC is the mediating agency of Canadian federalism, at any level short of the electorate. And yet, the parties approach this experience on an unequal basis, despite the equal sovereignty of each *en bloc*. In the traditional FMC, the central level has wielded by far the greater power.

Why should this be? The main reason is that the federal level speaks with one voice, while the provincial voice is fragmented. In truth, the federal level is internally diverse as well, but this never surfaces at the FMC table. All differences are brokered in advance to a single position. Typically the provincial level is hydra-headed and unbrokered. There is usually no monolithic "provincial position," even on matters that should be clearly "solidarity" issues for provinces, such as their role in the federation. In this environment, what normally happens is that the planned and united voice (Ottawa) runs circles around the chaotic voice (the provinces), through some mix of united strategy, and co-option of client states. I submit that the full potential of federalism requires a proper balance of forces. In short, and in the vernacular, the provinces need to get their act together if our country is to work well.

The second element of solution is to provide incentives to cooperation among the provinces. If it has not happened in the past, what need we do to make it happen in the future? The inducements are three — *positive, negative,* and *protective.* The positive side is the search for a better Canada. This is a noble (albeit minor, in *realpolitik*) incentive. The negative incentive is this: a good provincially-led solution will avoid national breakup, or the "neverendum" scenario. This should certainly focus the attention of the smaller provinces. And then there is one brand-new incentive that we should be willing to provide — a guarantee to the smaller provinces (subject, I would argue, to a lengthy sunset clause) of a principle of *no net deterioration in financial relationships* in a restructured federation.

The third element of solution is to improve — indeed, to *prove* de novo, as far as the general public is concerned — the possibility of effective provincial cooperation. The Courchene paper properly notes that the public does not believe in this possibility. That being the case, why even contemplate a province-based solution? There is a lot of credibility that has to be earned here, and I say that with apologies to provincial public servants, who know from their point of view that in fact genuine cooperation has been broadening and deepening at a considerable rate.

DETAILS

The challenge then becomes one of producing an interprovincial institution that is *continuous, bureaucratic, transparent, comprehensive, and accountable.* All of these attributes need some elaboration.

By *continuous* one means an ongoing organization that is not reinvented for each First Ministers' Conference and then dismantled. Only a continuous organization can develop an institutional memory, and memory is key to progress.

By *bureaucratic* one implies the best meaning of the word — orderly, reliable, with targets, a work plan, and performance measurement.

The concept of *transparent* goes directly to the worry about a "democratic deficit." All modern governance theory relies upon the fulsome dissemination of information to affected publics. Of course, this ethic flies squarely in the face of the current mode of intergovernmental relations, which is opaque, even secretive.

By *comprehensive* one wishes for an institution that would integrate *all* intergovernmental concerns and themes. Of course, many specific matters would ordinarily be handled as to substance on an ad hoc basis, or bilaterally, or by specialized councils — ministers of the environment, or education, or social policy, or interprovincial trade — but just as any government needs some kind of Cabinet office to keep track of things, a multigovernment network needs this even more so. (Of course, there is no suggestion here of comparable powers. A Cabinet office is the extension of an all-powerful first minister; there is no single such centre of power as between governments.)

And by *accountable* one again seeks to deal with the very important issue often called the "democratic deficit," which arises when there is an uncontrolled power centre. Indeed, the existing pattern of federal-provincial and interprovincial relations suffers from this sort of "deficit" to a very significant degree.

Transparency is one key. Intergovernmental relations are highly secretive at the moment, more for (very human) reasons of political and bureaucratic convenience than anything else. Specific ministerial accountability on intergovernmental matters to legislatures is another key. The ability of majority governments to speak for their legislatures is virtually untrammelled. That is not the problem. The problem is the practice of not even referring intergovernmental matters for *comment*, in advance of decision.

PROCEDURES

A modest beginning would best be made by a few "lead provinces" working together on an informal basis, in a few areas. Observers from other provinces should always be welcome as the new machinery grows, and accession by other provinces would be on their own timetables. The best way to go here is to take a lesson from the early development of the EU — to start small, with few members and limited objectives (coal, steel, and nuclear to start) and major safeguards (unanimous voting in all things, to start), and then build on success as people become comfortable with the process.

In the beginning, nothing need be formal at all, and no new goals need be set — simply the better working of existing intergovernmental relationships. This in itself would be a hugely useful first step, and requires nothing more than a handful of premiers asking their IGA Deputies (for example) to meet on a regular basis with an agenda, a workplan, and regular reports — always in accord with the *desiderata* of continuity, bureaucratic integrity, transparency, comprehensiveness, and accountability.

A MORE AMBITIOUS AGENDA

While the above modest evolution would be a useful step, it might not be enough in the current unity circumstances of Canada. In particular, there is no drama, no symbolic component that speaks clearly to a new federalism. The central government in Ottawa currently takes the position that it has done all that is required. I disagree.

If one thinks that something more is necessary, the proposals will most likely have to come from the provincial governments as the only other repositories of power and legitimacy. There exists, therefore, a need for a specific *acceptance of a provincial responsibility to develop jointly a proposal for a new federalism.* This would require tangible measures to give reality to the approach.

If anything is to happen, it will be by way of a small group of "lead provinces" — which would have to include at least two of the large provinces and two of the small. What would be the steps?

- *First*, a public commitment to produce new ideas for the federation.

- *Second*, reassurances — to the public, to other provinces — that the intent is not to advantage or disadvantage any region. In particular, specific assurances of fiscal fairness would need to be given to the smaller provinces.

- *Third*, process. As to a *public process*, the Canada West Foundation idea of an *interprovincial legislative committee* to talk to Canadians about what they want to see in an evolving Canada is a very promising one. As to *expert and bureaucratic process*, there is a need for a principled review of all governmental tasks, from the smallest village council to the largest federal ministry, based on the concept of *program review* (developed by the federal government for its own internal purposes) and *subsidiarity* (developed by the EU for its internal purposes).

The end result of this fundamental reexamination would be a new approach to the assignment of duties based on service to the public. And, of course, while this is not the proper forum for elaboration of details, questions of revenue and financing must always be central to such an examination.

• *Fourth*, while this process would be commenced by "lead provinces," others would be free to join as ready, and the active cooperation of the central government would be sought.

• *Fifth*, as all of the above would have important implications for the structure of federalism, it would be useful to have the (hopefully regularized) machinery of the Premiers' Conference and the First Ministers' Conference monitoring the process.

MONITORING AND ENFORCEMENT

The Courchene paper has little to say about monitoring. This is an important area, for information is what drives a democracy, in the end. The best monitoring device in measuring the delivery of social services is the machinery of the First Ministers' Conference (desirably, as upgraded as suggested in this paper), working closely with Statistics Canada.

The Courchene paper has a great deal to say about enforcement, and I will not attempt to add much to that, except to express a belief that as contractual relationships among governments having to do with the social union broaden and deepen, I have no doubt that governments will live up to their obligations. Why so? Because major default in social union agreements would cause a significant discontinuity in the rule of law, directly affecting a very large number of voters in the offending province. Since our whole society in the end is based on common sense and respect for the law, I think that any concerns exist only in theory.

CONCLUSION

The main problem in all of this discussion is not the end, but the means. The end may be "Courchene Canada," or something else. That is for people and their governments to determine over time.

But the *means* is central. The negotiation of an overall social contract is so massive that it is unlikely to happen in any human time frame, let alone the unity-constrained time frame of Canada. Therefore we will have to proceed by way of more incremental progress in substance, with more attention devoted to the machinery to get us there.

PART THREE

COMMENTARY

Reflections on ACCESS

Thomas J. Courchene

INTRODUCTION

It is a rare privilege to have a group of distinguished scholars and practitioners analyze and critique one's work and I am grateful to all for participating and to the Institute of Intergovernmental Relations for orchestrating the conference.

Perhaps I should not be so grateful, since if one were to compile the full set of criticisms of ACCESS aired here, precious little of the substance would be seen to survive. What this probably means (apart from the fact that few, if any, of the participants have bought unconditionally into the ACCESS model) is that much of the appeal of the paper lies elsewhere than in the precise substance. Indeed, Peter Meekison may have been close to the mark when he noted that ACCESS provides a timely and comprehensive catalyst for political scientists, economists, lawyers and practitioners to re-engage themselves in the re-making of Canadian *federalism* and at the same time to extricate themselves from more than a decade of Canadian *constitutionalism*. Whatever the role played by ACCESS, I welcome the opportunity to offer some reflections on the overall response to the paper since it appeared and, in particular, on the issues raised by conference participants.

These reflections fall into three related categories. The first set will provide somewhat more in the way of the rationale for ACCESS than appears in the paper itself. Just as various analysts have read different things into ACCESS, so too is the motivation multifaceted — embracing, among other perspectives, the positive (ACCESS is necessary to preserve social Canada) and the normative (ACCESS is desirable in its own right). This is not so much an attempt to bolster the normative arguments, since ardent centralists are unlikely to be persuaded, as it is to lend support to the positive case by situating ACCESS in the context of the emerging geoeconomic and political-economic reality in the upper half of North America.

The second set addresses some of the feedback and commentary on ACCESS since its release. In particular, special focus is directed to Premier John Savage's Empire Club speech in Toronto in October.

These perspectives provide an appropriate entrée to the core of this paper, namely responding to the conference proceedings. Since I will agree with many of the issues raised by participants, it may appear on occasion that I am conceding far too much substantive ground. However, it is important to recognize that the participants are frequently coming at ACCESS from highly different perspectives. The approach I took in the paper was to design a series of models in line with a dozen framework axioms. While I may or may not have succeeded in this exercise, the message from the seminar is that these framework axioms are rather narrow. For example, a proposal that scores high marks in terms of internalizing the externalities arising from the increasing interdependence among and between governments may (and probably will) score low in terms of Roger Gibbins' criteria of democracy and populism. It probably cannot be otherwise, since the many perspectives from which participants approach the paper are, in their pristine form, not mutually compatible. The point of this is to note that agreeing with the comments from the particular perspective within which they are conceived is, or at least can be, quite different than conceding substantive ground in terms of ACCESS.

By way of a final introductory comment, a few words on process are probably in order. Ontario was an active participant in the interprovincial process that led to the impressive *Report to Premiers,* the 15 key social policy principles which appear as Table 3 of the ACCESS paper (see Appendix). The Ontario government was then anxious to ensure that the social policy reform and renewal momentum associated with the *Report to Premiers* not be lost. Accordingly, the Ontario Ministry of Intergovernmental Affairs asked me to develop some alternative design and delivery mechanisms for social policy — alternatives to "federal unilateralism" in terms of the archetypes in the Figure 1 schema (adopted from the Canadian Policy Research Network). The first of these alternatives is the "interim" ACCESS model. This model is federal-provincial, would fall somewhere between the cooperative and collaborative categories of Figure 1, and is probably quite consistent with the philosophy underpinning the *Report to Premiers*. (This is a convenient place to admit that it was probably inappropriate to refer to this as the "interim" model, in the sense that interim necessarily implies some intermediate stopping point on the way to a final position. As many people have noted, the so-called interim model could, under certain conditions, end up as the long-term solution.) The "full" ACCESS model is much more interprovincial in nature, much more in line with the written constitutional word and would fall into the "provincial federalism" archetype of Figure 1.[1] In general, reference to ACCESS will refer to the "full" model. While the Ministry of Intergovernmental Affairs

FIGURE 1: Five Archetypes for the Social Union

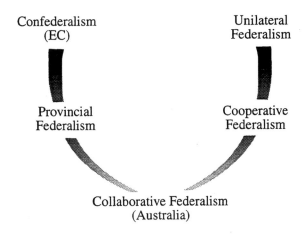

Source: Biggs 1996.

commissioned the paper and is one of the sponsors of this conference, the views and ideas in ACCESS and in what follows are my own and should not be attributed to the Ontario government.

MOTIVATING ACCESS

ACCESS can be rationalized (or critiqued, for that matter) in terms of both normative and positive arguments. The normative argument, namely that ACCESS is desirable in its own right, dominates most of the paper. In particular, the 12 framework axioms are intended to place a normative underpinning to ACCESS. Beyond this, a normative case can be built around other considerations — a division-of-powers perspective, a national-unity perspective as well as arguments to the effect that a full blown socio-economic union requires both horizontal, bottom-up integration as well as vertical, top-down integration.

However, as important in terms of motivating the ACCESS model are positive arguments, arguments premised on the notion that, under the status quo, the socio-economic union is beginning to fragment and that new approaches are needed to secure the east-west safety net. Underpinning these arguments is the recognition of a fundamental shift in the geoeconomic and political-economic environment of the Canadian federation. Much has been written to the effect that globalization and the knowledge-information revolution are tending to transfer powers upward (NAFTA, Europe 1992) and downward (to markets, citizens, and regions) from national governments of federal states. At the more general level, the most comprehensive reflection of the impact of the new order is that by sociologist Manuel Castells in his sure-to-be classic *The Rise of the Network Society*:

> The global economy emerging from information-based production and competition is characterized by its *interdependence*, its *asymmetry*, its *regionalization, the increasing diversification within each region*, its *selective inclusiveness*, its *exclusionary segmentation,* and, as a result of all these features, an extraordinarily *variable geometry* that tends to dissolve historical economic geography (1996, p. 106, emphasis in original).

These tendencies are dramatically enhanced for the Canadian federation because of our particular economic geography, among other things the increasing dominance of north-south over east-west trade as well as the likelihood that Ontario has finally recognized its role as, arguably, North America's premier economic region state (Courchene and Telmer 1997). Recent trade data relating to Ontario support both these assertions. Not only does Ontario export more than twice as much internationally as it does to other provinces ($130.4 billion versus $61.9 billion in 1995), but over the 1990-95 period international exports have grown nearly eight times as fast as interprovincial exports. On the import side, international integration is even stronger — international imports are nearly four times as large as interprovincial imports, with the former growing 12 times as fast since 1990 (Crane 1997).

The message that rings loud and clear here is that in the face of these pervasive centrifugal forces the centre will have increasing difficulty in guaranteeing an east-west socio-economic union. ACCESS recognizes this emerging geoeconomics and geopolitics of Canada within North America by focusing on new instruments to deliver our longstanding goals on the socio-economic front — instruments that are consistent with the new global economic order.

I must confess that I remain puzzled why so few analysts have accepted this vision of twenty-first century Canada. What is not puzzling, however, is that if one does not buy into this emerging vision then the inherent appeal of the full-blown ACCESS model will be reduced. The part of the positive argument for alternative approaches to fiscal federalism that analysts *have* accepted relates to the impact of federal fiscal restraint and deficit-shifting on the provinces. In effect, the federation is undergoing unprecedented fiscally-triggered decentralization (e.g., the 45,000 cut in the federal civil service; the transfer of tourism, recreation, mining, forestry, etc., to the provinces; Ottawa's voluntary restrictions on the exercise of the federal spending power; the devolution of training and of the development uses of Employment Insurance (EI); the elimination of several conditions embedded in the former Canada Assistance Plan; and the reduction in Canada Health and Social Transfer (CHST) cash transfers by close to 50 percent). But decentralization into what? There is no framework at the provincial level that can accommodate this unprecedented decentralization and at the same time preserve the east-west social safety net. Again a rationale for ACCESS. Indeed, as early as 1991, Ontario Premier Bob Rae became convinced that some new instruments were needed to "protect social programmes in the moves toward decentralization which were inevitable" and to maintain "the national glue" in a more devolved Canada (Rae 1996, p. 179). Rae's preferred solution was his "social charter." While ACCESS, unlike the social charter, stays well clear of the constitution, what they do have in common is mechanisms/instruments alternative to "federal unilateralism" in terms of preserving and promoting the social union.

To globalization and federal fiscal restraint as components of a positive case for ACCESS, one can probably add a third factor — the inequity associated with the 1990 cap on the Canada Assistance Plan (CAP), which has recently been carried over to the CHST. With cash transfers falling in any event, this discriminatory treatment of Alberta, British Columbia, and Ontario provides an incentive for the very provinces that have the fiscal wherewithal to begin marching to their own social policy drummer. For example, Alberta's budget *surplus* this fiscal year is well in excess of its cash transfers from Ottawa. These factors reinforce each other — globalization suggests that the traditional east-west links and bonds are becoming overwhelmed by north-south linkages, drastic reductions in federal cash transfers to the provinces weaken Ottawa's financial capacity and moral authority to impose east-west integration from above, and the perpetuation of the cap on CAP serves to hasten the day when the burden of federal unilateralism (or the lack of provincial flexibility) exceeds the benefits of the cash transfers.

My ranking of the importance of these factors would place globalization well in front, both because of its pervasiveness and because of its irreversibility. As already noted, I suspect that most others would attach more importance to the fiscal factors. In turn this allows them (and Milne in particular) to downplay the positive case for ACCESS on (admittedly plausible) grounds that Ottawa's fiscal position is rapidly improving and that the above fiscal pressures may be reversible. This will be addressed later.

While still focusing on pre-conference reflections, I now turn to some substantive issues that have come to the fore, beginning with Premier John Savage's critique.

THE "TWO CANADAS" DEBATE

On 15 October 1996, Nova Scotia Premier John Savage delivered a powerful address to Toronto's Empire Club — "The Two Canadas: The Devolution Debate."[2] The importance of the message, as well as the fact it complements many of the participants' views, merits quotation at length:

> this brings me to my theme, Two Canadas: The Devolution Debate. What I have in mind here are not the uneasy relations between Quebec and the rest of the country, or even the contentious issues that beset aboriginal/non-native dealings. I'm referring to the Canada that has and the Canada that has not...

> Most recently, the Two Canadas asserted themselves in August at the First Ministers' Meeting when, as Newfoundland Brian Tobin so succinctly put it, "Courchene was thrown from the train."

> While not on the official agenda, Professor Thomas Courchene's controversial paper on re-balancing federal-provincial social responsibilities gave us a defining moment. For the first time Nova Scotia and five other have-not provinces voiced a resounding and harmonious "no" to an option that obviously has some appeal to Canada's rich provinces. We said "no" to the Courchene scenario in which Ottawa would completely get out of social programs like health care and turn its cash transfers into equalized tax points for the provinces.

> The fact that Have-Canada, particularly Ontario and Alberta, would even bring Courchene's provocative paper along as a non-agenda item is troubling. It suggests that the richer members of our Canadian family are out of touch with their poorer relations; that Ontario and Alberta don't fully appreciate the full implications of what Courchene is suggesting...

> The plain truth is Nova Scotia can't afford to let Ottawa vacate the social welfare field because, on its own, our province doesn't have the money to bankroll a takeover. Ontario, Alberta and British Columbia do. Consequently, we still see a role for the federal government in developing national standards, provided they are achieved in consensus with the provinces...

> ...we've been able to keep them [our social programs] ... because of a system of federal equalization payments *which have been coupled with cash transfers for social programs with built-in equalization factors.*

> Ontario argues that these equalization factors should be scrapped from our social programs and integrated into the formula for equalization payments. We can't go along with that idea; we'd be financial losers in the formula's renegotiation and we know it. Courchene's scenario, turning cash transfers into equalized tax points, falls short of the mark, too. Our social programs would suffer. They couldn't be sustained

in an equitable way with Ontario's programs, Alberta's or British Columbia's (1996, pp. 2-3, second italics added).

This critique raises several key challenges to ACCESS — challenges made more important by virtue of the fact that they emanate from the premier.

I want to begin with the issue of the "two Canadas." I accept the fact that the have versus have-not issue has come to the fore of late. While this is most unfortunate, it has, with respect, little or nothing to do with ACCESS. Rather, the tension arises from the overall federal transfer cuts on the one hand and the discriminatory treatment arising from the cap on CAP on the other. The cap on CAP so outraged Bob Rae that he hinted that, unless Ottawa moved to restore equity in financing, the entire equalization program could be placed in the balance. But in the above quote, Premier Savage argues that Nova Scotia actually requires that there be equalizing components in social programs other than the formal equalization formula. I can think of few initiatives more likely to erode the east-west sharing commitment than a continuation of inserting distributional (provincial/regional) components in every federal program. The ACCESS approach is to address any provincial funding deficiencies by altering the formal equalization program rather than by altering the various social programs themselves.

Relatedly, the premier claims that his province will lose from any switch from cash transfers to tax point transfers. This does not follow at all. There are really two issues here — (i) the distribution of revenues between Ottawa and the provinces and (ii) the distribution of revenues across provinces. In terms of the former, one advantage of tax-point transfers is that they become *provincial* revenues and, therefore, no longer subject to unilateral federal cuts and caps and freezes. Moreover, by the very definition of tax-point transfers, they will grow with income so that tax-point transfers will eventually dominate virtually any cash transfer floor. Thus, part of the rationale for tax points was to *increase* the monies going to the provinces relative to the status quo.[3]

How this increase is allocated across provinces is a separate issue. If these tax points were equalized under the existing (five-province-standard) equalization formula, then they would indeed be worth more to Ontario than to Nova Scotia (although Nova Scotia could still be better off vis-à-vis the status quo because overall provincial revenues could be greater). But they could also be equalized to the level of the top province, as was the case for the EPF tax-point transfers and is the case for the CHST tax-point transfers.[4]

ACCESS is silent on all of this and, I think, appropriately so. It may well be that Premier Savage believes that the have-not provinces will lose out in terms of any negotiations pursuant to a tax-point transfer under ACCESS. If so, then Nova Scotia would presumably also lose out even in the absence of ACCESS (and, indeed, as currently appears to be occurring in the scaling down of EI and the move to eliminate the CHST allocation differentials). Thus, I find no substance in the premier's claim, although it may make good politics in terms of attempting to prevent Ottawa from removing the current preferential CHST treatment for Nova Scotia, and the have-not provinces generally.

This may be the appropriate point in the analysis to draw attention to a recent paper by Boothe and Hermanutz, "Paying for ACCESS: Financing Government in a Decentralized Canada" (1997). The authors accept the overall expenditure and taxation principles in ACCESS, embed them within a more general tax- and expenditure-assignment model and then simulate alternative scenarios for financing the federation. Their conclusion is that under ACCESS, the federal-provincial "shifts in expenditures and revenues are less dramatic than one might expect." Efforts like that of Boothe and Hermanutz go a long way to rescue me from David Cameron's summary reflection that there was insufficient fiscal detail in ACCESS. More importantly, these sorts of analyses are valuable even without ACCESS since the system is decentralizing in any event and we need to get some handle on what this might mean for federal and provincial finances. And for those that feel that these financial implications may get in the way of the substance of ACCESS-type structural reform, there is always Gordon Gibson's recommendation:

> there is one brand new incentive that we should be willing to provide — a guarantee to the smaller provinces (subject, I would argue, to a lengthy sunset clause) of a principle of *no net deterioration in financial relationships* in a restructured federation (italics added).

Finally, when delivering this paper in various parts of the country (although admittedly mostly in the have provinces), among the first questions from the audience is: What's in this for the have provinces? Yet several participants, as well as Premier Savage, take it almost as a matter of faith that ACCESS was tailored for the benefit of the have provinces. In fact, I would venture a guess that ACCESS would be more advantageous to the have-not provinces. One aspect of this is Gordon Gibson's perspective, namely that a "good provincially led solution would avoid a national breakup or a 'neverendum' scenario" which, in turn, is in the clear interests of the smaller provinces. The more straightforward point is that it is the richer provinces that have both the ability and the incentive to go their own way on the social union. This being the case, it would appear to be in the interests of the poorer provinces to find mechanisms by which the rich provinces will commit themselves to an east-west social contract. ACCESS is one such mechanism. To ignore this argument is tantamount to asserting that Ottawa will always be able to address fully the needs and aspirations of the have-not provinces. I think that this way of conceptualizing Canada is over. Indeed, as I have argued elsewhere

(1994), recognition that this era was likely over was a key catalyst to Premier Frank McKenna's "re-engineering" of New Brunswick.

While I shall return to aspects of Premier Savage's speech, especially his assessment of what transpired at Jasper, in the concluding section of the paper, I turn now to some of the important issues aired in the conference. What follows makes no claim to be either a comprehensive or integrative overview: this task has been admirably accomplished by David Cameron.

CONFERENCE PROCEEDINGS: SELECTED COMMENTS

Session I: Burelle and Swinton

André Burelle's "Pact on the Canadian Social and Economic Union" has nearly as much claim as my previous writings to be the intellectual underpinning of ACCESS. Not surprisingly, therefore, I agree with most of Burelle's comments in terms of how a convention or pact might operate. For example, it is undoubtedly true that the intergovernmental decision rules would vary across areas — from unanimity in terms of truly confederal areas to a simple majority rule when the issues are inherently federal.

More penetrating is Burelle's point that ACCESS has "chartist" or rights-based overtones. In part, it clearly does and this sets up an unavoidable tension between provincial flexibility on the one hand and pan-Canadian rights on the other. What is interesting in terms of the conference is that so many participants tended, like Burelle, to feel that ACCESS went too far in terms of pan-Canadianism. (Intriguingly, the press has taken the opposite approach, viewing ACCESS as a very decentralist document, i.e., as favouring provincial flexibility.) David Milne was most eloquent on this issue:

> Perhaps the greatest irony in this paper's bold defence of decentralized federalism is that it should offer so very little scope and promise for independent action by provincial communities without supervision by a central authority of some kind, whether federal, federal-provincial or interprovincial. If this is what federalism has come to, then perhaps we have lost our way.

Roger Gibbins comes at this same issue from a different vantage point:

> The problem stems from the combination of decentralization and intergovernmentalism in the ACCESS models, a combination that moves political decisions out of legislatures and into forms relatively insulated from public pressure, partisan debate and electoral combat.... [Premier] Klein has argued that decentralization should mean greater programmatic autonomy for provincial governments, and not the

entanglement of provincial governments in intergovernmental fora and agreements. We should, he suggests, trust provincial governments and bite the decentralization bullet.

Admittedly, ACCESS is vague, in part deliberately so, on where to draw the line between flexibility and pan-Canadianism since they are competing "goods" as it were. In terms of ensuring provincial flexibility, ACCESS builds on framework axioms #7 (competitive federalism), #10 (duality and asymmetry) and #11 (provincial treatment) while citizens rights flow directly from framework axiom #5. One way to approach this tension would be to argue that the rights that citizens would have under ACCESS are *between-province, not within-province, rights.* Thus, the rights would relate to the social *union,* not to the social *policies* of individual provincial governments. This would mean that "provincial treatment" would be the operational social union principle in much the same manner as "national treatment" underpins the Free Trade Agreement (FTA) and North American Free Trade Agreement (NAFTA).

While this may well be appropriate in terms of the economic side of ACCESS, it falls well short on the social side. The problem is that such an approach departs dramatically from the status quo and from what most Canadians (regardless of province of residence) hold near and dear in the social policy realm. For example, the *Canada Health Act* (CHA) embodies both social-union (e.g., portability) and social-policy (e.g., universality) principles. Thus, the dilemma facing ACCESS should be frustratingly clear. ACCESS is an instrument or institutional innovation for governance and integration in an increasingly decentralized federation. As such, it is consistent with a range of overarching goals. If I opt for the conception of the full-blown ACCESS model as embodying solely (or even principally) social-union principles, then the model will be seen to be abandoning aspects of the five existing CHA principles. And if the model incorporates fully the CHA principles, then ACCESS falls prey (appropriately) to the concerns of Burelle, Milne, and Gibbins. (Indeed, in this case, centralists should jump on the ACCESS bandwagon since it presents an alternative route to maintaining the status quo, when in actual fact the status quo is eroding.) There is no way of escaping this dilemma, especially since it is likely the case that the nature of the design and monitoring instrument itself will ultimately influence the outcome.

In the paper, I proffered a guess that in the health-care area the ongoing evolution is in the direction of the continental European model — a more comprehensive model but one that allows some role for ability-to-pay financing in all aspects of the system. One reason for this is that Canadians are becoming increasingly aware of the importance of well-being as distinct from the much narrower vision of health care (medicare, hospitalization). The CHA principles apply only to the latter: they do not cover home care, long-term care, nor services relating to wellness or well-being. My hunch is that citizens will opt for this more comprehensive approach — a Canada Well-Being Act, as it were, replete with its own set of principles — and that while these new principles will likely resemble the five CHA principles they will accommodate more provincial flexibility. It is hard to envision such a shift without the provinces playing a dominant role.

In any event, the essential point is that my vision of ACCESS (the "full" model) would embody more than simply portability and social *union* issues: it would incorporate principles relating to within-province social policy. The shared values and the sharing-community nature of Canada suggests that Canadians will want some minimum standards/principles to be part of any convention on the social union. As noted in the ACCESS paper, neither Ottawa nor Canadians would commit to this model without the existence of such binding commitments. Nor should they.

Where I part company with Burelle is with respect to his claim that ACCESS cannot be a "win-win" package because, in its present form, it is not acceptable to the majority of Quebecers. In response, I shall make four brief points. First, this paper is, at base, not about how to reintegrate Quebec into the Canadian family. Rather it is about how the Canadian federation might respond to the challenges emerging in the millennium. Nonetheless (and second), ACCESS does resonate quite well in Quebec, at least from the feedback that I have received from Quebecers. Third, and following on the previous point, it would have been possible to have written the ACCESS paper from a pro-Quebec or at least a more-Quebec vantage point. As the paper stands, except for framework axiom #10 (duality and asymmetry), which does recognize aspects of Quebec's specificity, there are almost no specific references to Quebec. By way of a summary fourth point, let me agree with Burelle's ultimate goal but then suggest that ACCESS is an appropriate means towards this end. Following the approach of the Group of 22 (1996), what Canadians and Canadian federalism need now is some tangible evidence that our system can be seen to be flexible and responsive or, in terms I utilized elsewhere (1996), can be rebalanced and revitalized. More to the point, it is precisely in the context of a successfully evolving federal institutional structure that issues such as the recognition of Quebec's distinctiveness become much easier. Because such recognition is asymmetrical, ACCESS can be an important catalyst since it too will surely generate significant asymmetries.

Katherine Swinton began her comments by making a point that was echoed by most participants — namely that ACCESS, conceived and implemented as one umbrella convention with a series of subaccords, is too much like mega-constitution reform of the Charlottetown variety or like full-blown "summit federalism." Not only should the preferred approach be incremental, but it ought to be "functional" as well. In terms of the latter, this calls for reliance on a large variety of models — depending on the function in question, the appropriate model might involve standard setting, it might rely on delegation or it might be defined by acceptable *processes*. Surely, everyone would agree with all of this. Yet one might still refer to the accumulated set of incremental and functional agreements as "ACCESS" in much the same way that the scores of incremental and functional integration directives in the EU are referred to as *Europe 1992*.

Swinton then turns her attention to the issue of ensuring that intergovernmental agreements are binding and enforceable. This is an area that merits further research, especially since we are in an era where intergovernmental agreements are likely to proliferate. I was especially intrigued by Swinton's suggestion that one might try to lend priority to some elements of a convention that might serve to make them, as in the case of human rights codes, susceptible to enforcement through adjudication by the courts and by John Whyte's hint that some equivalent to section 51 (xxxvii) of the Australian constitution (quoted in ACCESS) may, if triggered by some reference to "national concerns," fall under "Peace, Order and Good Government." Fully one-third of the ACCESS paper was devoted to issues relating to compliance, enforcement, and remedies. But I am largely a consumer of ideas in this area (and Swinton was one of the principal producers I drew upon). Some intellectual/institutional entrepreneur ought to enlist the constitutional scholars to expand our knowledge base in this important area.

Session II: Milne and Leslie

David Milne and Peter Leslie, in quite different ways, engage ACCESS in terms of its political-federal underpinnings. Milne begins by challenging the notion of *inevitability* and *irreversibility* that underpins the ACCESS model.[4] In particular, Milne challenges the fiscal determinism aspect of ACCESS by pointing out that, at long last, one can foresee the "makings of a monumental [federal] fiscal turnaround unthinkable for decades." Therefore, the federal spending power will again soon be alive and well and the federal government will again be in the social policy driver's seat.

This is an important observation and one that has been raised by various commentators. While it is far from obvious that Ottawa is out of the fiscal woods (e.g., the $5 billion it pockets from EI premiums are not, at least yet, deemed to be permanent federal revenues), let me accept the Milne proposition that the feds will become fiscally flush. Can Ottawa then use its fiscal freedom to re-centralize power (reinvigorate federal unilateralism) on the social policy front? Not easily, for at least two reasons. First, while Ottawa may well see a recovery in terms of dollars, it is much less likely that it would or could ever recover the powers it is in the process of signing away in terms of training and the developmental uses of EI. Second, it is highly unlikely that Ottawa would use its fiscal flexibility to reverse its earlier unilateral behaviour with respect to cash transfers to the provinces.

Rather, it would in all likelihood either move into a high visibility area replete with new federal standards/principles or work in its own jurisdiction. In this context, the ongoing federal-provincial deliberations over a new child tax benefit potentially falls into both of the above categories since, in the final analysis, Ottawa can always enrich the existing child benefit. The point is not only that a restoration of federal dollars is no guarantee that recent events are "reversible" but that any new federal initiatives in areas of provincial jurisdiction are almost surely to involve provincial co-determination. If Ottawa wants to renege on its 1996 Throne Speech commitments, the Annual Premiers' Conference in Jasper will ensure that it cannot.

Milne also raises the obvious (and difficult) question: Why would Ottawa agree to ACCESS? As Milne points out, there is no incentive for Ottawa to "abdicate" its traditional role in the social policy arena. But Ottawa has voluntarily agreed to constrain its exercise of the spending power and it is in the process of signing bilateral agreements with the provinces for the devolution of training and of the developmental uses of EI. What was Ottawa's incentive to "abdicate" its traditional role here? To be sure, part of the answer may relate to Quebec and the national unity issue. But I believe the pressures go deeper. Federalism is not only about the division of powers: it is also about process. And the policy interdependencies, both between and across governments, are becoming so pervasive that a workable Canadian federation requires new processes, especially in light of the north-south forces. The two levels of government have several issues that they are currently grappling with: harmonization of the GST and the PSTs, the CPP/QPP, a new child benefits package, the transfer of securities regulation to Ottawa, etc. All of these involve both levels of government and all are currently in limbo because our federation is weak on the process dimension. This is surprising in the sense that for much of the postwar period we Canadians excelled in terms of breathing creative process into written constitutional word (Courchene 1995). The current impasse is in no small way the legacy of nearly two decades of focus on constitutionalism (i.e., *structure*) at the expense of political/ institutional evolution (i.e., *process*). In any event, the answer to Milne's query is that Ottawa simply cannot avoid embracing greater "intergovernmentalism" as the necessary response to the growing (and, in my view, irreversible) policy interdependencies between and among the two levels of government. While this may not mean ACCESS, this model is nonetheless one variant of enhanced intergovernmentalism.

Peter Leslie's focus is on political feasibility or, rather, the lack of it in the ACCESS proposal. He begins by arguing that provinces would be reluctant to sign on to a convention that had any substance. (The best response to this is to note that the sovereign nation states of the EU have, reluctant or otherwise, signed on to intergovernmental conventions with plenty of substance and teeth.) Leslie then advances a model that, in his view, *has* political feasibility. The key feature borrows from an earlier proposal by Hobson and St-Hilaire (1994), more recently adopted by Maslove (1996), which would convert cash transfers into tax points in the form of a tax abatement rather than (as in ACCESS) a formal transfer of tax room. Thus, the value of these tax points would be earmarked for a specific social policy fund which both Leslie, Hobson/St-Hilaire, and Maslove would allocate to the provinces on an equal-per-capita basis (as, indeed, the existing tax points under the CHST are effectively allocated). Basically, this is the financial equivalent to adopting the $11 billion cash floor, indexing it by the growth in the value of a tax point and then distributing the proceeds on an equal-per-capita basis. To be sure, this is more generous than the status quo. But Leslie's proposal resembles the status quo in that it binds the provinces, but it does not bind Ottawa: it would be monitored by "Parliament or any federal minister" and could be terminated after giving three year's notice and the tax abatements would then revert back to the federal government. This is federal unilateralism. It is the antithesis of ACCESS. While Leslie's model would have had much to offer as a preferred alternative to the existing set of EPF/CAP arrangements, it really does not address the underlying issue that ACCESS is grappling with. Given that Leslie's solution is not in tune with one of the key goals of ACCESS, it is perhaps not surprising that he is also not onside with the ACCESS solution.

Leslie also asks whether Quebec would or could remain outside a socioeconomic union. In ACCESS, I took it for granted that all provinces would eventually sign on. Why would Quebec prefer to maintain the status quo when its powers, flexibility and finances would be enhanced under ACCESS? Indeed, even a PQ government would probably have to give serious consideration to ACCESS. This is so because, under ACCESS, the preservation of the economic union and social union comes, in part at least, under the auspices of an interprovincial agreement. This is precisely the sort of agreement that the PQ wants to strike if and when it becomes sovereign. If Quebec is not willing to be part of the socioeconomic union while it is part of Canada, why would the provinces allow Quebec in, if and when it is no longer a part of Canada?

Finally, Peter's reference to aspects of ACCESS are "pure fantasy, based on serious confusion as to what is involved in maintaining common standards in social policy" was no doubt intended to trigger a response. The issue at hand relates to an apparent inconsistency since, paraphrasing Leslie, on the one hand, I presume that public opinion will demand that provinces adopt common standards and, on the other, also presume that if province A gets away with reneging on its commitments in any given area, public support for maintaining standards could wither in other provinces and this fear will lead the other provinces to insist that province A toes the line. I fail to see the supposed inconsistency here, since this is precisely the behaviour that ensued in the recent Ottawa-Alberta dust-up over medicare. All other provinces wanted Ottawa to enforce the CHA principles, since failure to do so would generate pressures (both external and internal) that would make it much more difficult to hold the line in their own provinces (even though a majority of their citizens might be in favour of holding the line). This is the familiar "race to the bottom" scenario, where the final equilibrium is decidedly inferior to the starting point. Leslie also challenges the concept of "contagion" and, in particular, the view that a few key provinces can trigger a process that will ensure that the rest of the provinces will be brought on board. But isn't this exactly what is happening in the ongoing child benefit negotiations, where the lead provinces are British Columbia and Saskatchewan and the file is being advanced by Alberta (as this year's Chair of the APC). In the broader context, this child benefit process is especially instructive since the provinces will be fully involved in developing and (I would guess) monitoring the common standards. This is the post-Jasper world. Indeed, it carries the process or intergovernmental dimension so far that the governments have apparently struck a deal without full knowledge of the ultimate substance. In any event, not only would it be difficult to imagine a development more fully in line in both timing and substance with the interim model: ACCESS is back on the train, while some of its critics have been left in the station.

In the discussion period Ken Norrie raised an interesting dilemma. He began by noting that Ottawa provides us with more in the way of national standards than some Canadians want and that hidden or implicit equalization also results in more equalization than some of us want. But, and here is the intriguing issue, if we reduce the *role* or *number* or *level* of national standards, do we at the same time diminish the rationale for equalization? With the relaxing of the standards in the welfare area, we appear to be already engaged in the process of decreasing the role of national standards. Thus, the easy way out for me is to use this welfare example to assert that, interesting as this issue is, it transcends ACCESS. But it probably does provide an overarching argument for have-not provinces to champion the notion of national standards and it does suggest that without incorporating some within-province social policy principles, ACCESS will never obtain the imprimatur of the have-not provinces.

Session III: Gibbins and Gibson

Roger Gibbins raises a fascinating range of issues associated with enhanced "intergovernmentalism" as a governance instrument:

- intergovernmentalism favours interstate over intrastate federalism;

- intergovernmentalism diffuses electoral accountability, as traditionally defined;

- intergovernmentalism represents a retreat from populism;

- intergovernmentalism is a retreat from democratic government; and, addressed earlier,

- intergovernmentalism may stand in the way of real decentralization.

In greater or lesser degrees, all of these propositions ring true as criticisms of ACCESS.

The problem with these criticisms is that they transcend ACCESS in the sense that they are likely to be applicable to much of the evolution of governance in the millennium. This is so because globalization and the knowledge-information revolution are not only influencing the geoeconomic and political-economic forces in the federation; they are also having a major impact on the political-democracy-sovereignty underpinnings of nation states. For starters, traditional sovereignty is, like powers, being transferred upwards, outwards, and downwards from central governments of federal nation states. That is, it is becoming increasingly distributed or, to take George Bush's phrase out of context, sovereignty is becoming "a thousand points of light." In part, this is because governance in the emerging integrated economic order will progressively involve *contractual arrangements* with international organizations, with other nations, with business groups, with domestic organizations, with subnational governments, and so on. This is the executive federalism model writ large to apply across the board. Intergovernmentalism is just one subset of this increasing "executivism" of government. And from this follow virtually all of Gibbins' concerns. For example, executivism and intergovernmentalism, almost by definition, (a) are not populist and (b) create democracy deficits because decisions are frequently made in a forum beyond the jurisdiction of any individual voter.

What ought we to do about this? I have two polar comments. The first is that there is bound to be some scope in any proposal, ACCESS included, to ensure that the parameters are modified to embody aspects of these political concerns. For example, by conscious design the intergovernmental conventions in ACCESS depart from those of the Agreement on International Trade (AIT) variety. Specifically, under ACCESS (but not under the AIT) *individuals* can trigger the dispute resolution mechanism. Moreover, in terms of the proposed agreement relating to mutual recognition of skills accreditation across provinces, the burden of proof is assumed to rest with the parties to the accord, (i.e., governments) not with citizens. In simpler language, skills presumed to be transferable and accreditable unless governments can demonstrate to the contrary. These measures were designed explicitly to enhance democracy and populism alike and, relatedly, were intended to correct some of the deficiencies of the AIT.

The second comment will no doubt be viewed as an unwarranted exercise in discipline extraterritorially: political science needs to integrate the emerging reality with its traditional approaches to issues like sovereignty, citizenship, democracy, and populism. To associate these concepts with the nation state when the world is integrating and when citizens (thanks to the informatics revolution of which they are the principal beneficiaries) can and do have influences well beyond their state's borders (e.g., Greenpeace) is progressively inappropriate. David Held, among others, has begun grappling with this issue:

> In a world of interconnected political authorities and power centres, how should democracy be understood? Can the idea of a democratic polity or state be sustained in the face of systemic challenges from above and below? ... what is, and ought to be, the meaning of democracy in the context of the changing enmeshment of the local, national, regional and global? (1995, pp. 135-36).

Because the Canadian economy was so open, Canadian economists played a lead role in the development of the literature relating to the international economy. The Canadian polity is also far more "open" than the US polity so perhaps we can be leaders here as well. Elkins (1995) may be showing us the way.

In an important sense, I feel most at home in terms of Gordon Gibson's concluding paper. Gibson does not care whether the goal is a "Courchene Canada" or a "Burelle Canada." Rather he is interested in how we get from here to there: the key issue is "process" — the machinery needed to get wherever it is that we want to go. One of Gibson's most penetrating points is to argue that any interprovincial institution must be continuous, bureaucratic, transparent, comprehensive, and accountable (terms that he elaborates upon). Intriguingly, the provinces are moving in this direction with their APC (Annual Premiers' Conference) and the APC is probably more advanced on these scores than is the FMC. Obviously, I welcome Gibson's endorsement of the role that can be played by "lead provinces," which probably must number at least four with at least two from the have-not category. This is close to the concept of "contagion" in ACCESS.

Finally, and here I am probably putting words in Gibson's mouth, ACCESS is important not because of what we might achieve if we eventually got there, but because it is inherently process-, instrument- or machinery-oriented rather than "final-outcome" oriented. In a sense, this was the *raison d'être* of my paper. Globalization *et al.* may or may not alter the goals that we set for ourselves as a society. But they will certainly alter the nature of the means or the options that we can fall back upon to implement these goals. I think that Gibson would agree that the potential contribution of ACCESS to Canadian political economy is in terms of its *means* rather than its *ends*.

CONCLUSION

I have two closing comments. One relates to the John Savage notion that the "defining moment" at Jasper was that Nova Scotia and five other have-not provinces vetoed a proposal that, in his view, had some appeal to Canada's rich provinces. While Premier Savage was there and I was not, this is not what I would label as the defining moment at Jasper. What Jasper did was finally put paid to the unilateral federalism era of Canadian social policy history. The provinces launched themselves into a new era, one that resonates much more with ACCESS than with the status quo. For example, recommendation eight of the premiers' communique (of which Premier Savage was a signator) reads:

> It is recommended that Premiers direct their designates to the Federal/Provincial/ Territorial Council to design options for mechanisms and processes to develop and promote adherence to national principles and standards, for review by Premiers within six months. Both provincial/territorial and federal/provincial territorial options should be identified together with the issues best addressed by each of these options.

This recommendation goes beyond the "interim" model and, effectively, embraces aspects of the full ACCESS model.

The final comment is that the time has come for me to uncouple my link to ACCESS. It has had a marvellous launch and it has obtained a wide hearing and evaluation. This being said, however, it seems progressively unproductive for me to attempt to defend it in the face of all comers. Essentially, it must now fly (or not fly) on its own. Accordingly, and as I also noted in my concluding comments at the conference, I hereby grant one and all full access and all property rights to ACCESS.

NOTES

1. In a recent article, Judith Maxwell (1997) places the "full" ACCESS model into the "confederalism" archetype of Table 1. Surely this is wrong. I thought I was careful to argue that, even under the most extreme circumstances, important aspects of social policy would remain under Ottawa's control (drug testing, the immigration-health overlap, the progressivity of the income tax, elderly benefits, child tax credits, etc.). Initially, I had thought that the mutual recognition of skills accreditation might qualify as an area where only the provinces would be involved. But even here, one of Canada's major training institutions (the Canadian Forces) would have to be brought into the accreditation procedures and this means bringing in the federal government. Thus, "provincial federalism," not "confederalism" is where the full ACCESS model belongs. This aside, Maxwell's article is a most welcome contribution.

2. While Premier Savage's paper does not feature in any of the formal papers of this volume, the paper, its key ideas, and its implications did play a role in the roundtable discussions.

3. However, it is important to note that conversion to tax-point transfers will, over time, *not* increase the provinces' share of overall personal income tax revenues. Rather, it will ensure that the provincial share remains constant. This is so because of the total 100 tax points (a tax point is 1 percent of federal income tax) Ottawa will still retain the largest proportion and they too will increase in value as income increases.

4. Thus, I do not understand Peter Leslie's suggestion that if these tax points were to be equalized to the level of the highest-income province, then this would "probably require fundamental redesign of the fiscal arrangements." This is the status quo for the CHST tax points. What is true is that the number of tax points that a given amount of cash transfers would convert to would be smaller the more "equalizing" is the equalization. Perhaps the point is that, with ACCESS in place, the equalization program will remain the only federal transfer and that pressures will be mounted by the recipient provinces for equalizing all revenues, not just those associated with the former CHST, to the level of the highest province.

5. Among other issues, he notes that global forces are nothing if not complex and may point simultaneously in a centralizing and decentralizing direction. This is surely correct. For example, one would expect the most mobile of areas to be transferred upward. Indeed, in its 1996 budget, Ontario does propose that Ottawa play a greater role in the management of Canada's capital markets.

REFERENCES

Bigg, M. (1996), *Building Blocks for Canada's New Social Union*, Working Paper No. F02. (Ottawa: Canadian Policy Research Networks).

Boothe, P. and D. Hermanutz (1997), "Paying for ACCESS: Financing Government in a Decentralized Canada," in *The Nation State in a Global/ Information Era*, ed. T.J. Courchene (Kingston: The John Deutsch Institute for the Study of Economic Policy, Queen's University).

Castells, M. (1996), *The Rise of the Network Society* (Cambridge, MA.: Blackwells).

Courchene, T.J. (1994), *Social Canada in the Millennium* (Toronto: C.D. Howe Institute).

———— (1995), *Celebrating Flexibility: An Interpretive Essay on the Evolution of Canadian Federalism*, 1995 Benefactor's Lecture (Toronto: C.D. Howe Institute).

———— (1996), "In Quest of a New National Policy," in *Quebec-Canada: What is the Path Ahead?*, ed. J. Trent, R. Young, and G. Lachapelle (Ottawa: University of Ottawa Press).

Courchene, T.J. and C. Telmer (1997), *Ontario: From Heartland to Region Nature State* (forthcoming).

Crane, D. (1997), "Trade Patterns Eroding Our Nation," *The Toronto Star*, 5 January, p. F2.

Elkins, D.J. (1995), *Beyond Sovereignty: Territory and Political Economy in the Twenty-First Century* (Toronto: University of Toronto Press).

Held, D. (1995), *Democracy and the Global Order: From the Modern State to Cosmopolitan Governance* (Stanford: Stanford University Press).

Group of 22 (1966), "Making Canada Work Better," unpublished mimeo.

Hobson, P. and F. St-Hilaire (1994), *Reforming Federal-Provincial Fiscal Arrangements: Toward Sustainable Federalism* (Montreal: Institute for Research in Public Policy).

Maslove, A.M. (1996), *National Goals and the Federal Role in Health Care* (Ottawa: National Forum on Health).

Maxwell, J. (1996), "Governing Canada's Social Union," *Canadian Business Economics* 5(1):15-19.

Rae, B. (1996), *From Protest To Power* (Toronto: Viking).

Savage, J. (1996), "The Two Canadas: The Devolution Debate," speech to Toronto's Empire Club, 15 October.

APPENDIX

ACCESS: *A* Convention on the Canadian *E*conomic and *S*ocial *S*ystems

Thomas J. Courchene

I: INTRODUCTION

The last decade has wrought dramatic changes upon the Canadian and global economies alike. While the forces ushering in these changes have in general been beyond the control of any one country, their impacts have been most pronounced in terms of "domestic" policy arenas and nowhere more so than in the area of the welfare state. For example, globalization has internationalized production with obvious implications for the conception and role of the traditional welfare state. Typically, welfare states have been geared to their "national production machines:" when production becomes international, the structure and incentives of welfare states need to be rethought. Likewise, the advent of the information revolution and the emergence of knowledge as a key component in international competitiveness are serving to alter the social structure of developed nations. Market incomes are polarizing and non-standard jobs are proliferating, again with serious problems for old-style welfare states. Indeed, key aspects of societal structure are also undergoing substantial change: domestic unions are proving no match for international capital and production.

Within this context, which applies to all developed countries, Canada has some special challenges. With the increasing shift toward north-south, rather than east-west, trade all provinces except PEI now export more to the rest of the world than

ACCESS: A Convention on the Canadian Economic and Social Systems is a Working Paper prepared for the Ministry of Intergovernmental Affairs, Government of Ontario. It is reprinted by permission of the ministry.

to the rest of Canada (Courchene, 1996, Table 1). One obvious challenge arising from this is that our east-west transfer system must now be superimposed over an increasingly north-south trading system. Another is the resulting pressures for greater decentralization (and presumably enhanced asymmetry) that are mounting in the face of this shift from domestic to international markets. Finally, but hardly exhaustively, Canada's fiscal (debt/deficit) overhang is leading to a significant downsizing and decentralization of Ottawa's powers, especially in the social policy arena.

The consequence of all of this is that Canadians have never been so concerned about the future of their east-west social policy network. Phrases like "the end of Medicare" and a "race to the bottom" have become commonplace in spite of the fact that during the recent free-trade debate and election our social envelope was heralded as the cornerstone of much of our identity in the upper half of North America.

This is the backdrop to the ensuing analysis, which focusses on preserving and promoting the Canadian economic and social union. More explicitly, the paper proceeds from an assumption and a question, both drawn from the above scenario. The assumption is that social policy is undergoing substantial, indeed unprecedented, decentralization and the question is: how, in light of this decentralization, do we Canadians reconstitute our internal common markets in the socioeconomic arenas? The concise and inescapable answer is that the provinces have to be brought more fully and more formally into the key societal goal of preserving and promoting social Canada.

At the more detailed level, and as the (admittedly forced) title suggests, the proposed answer is ACCESS — *a convention on the Canadian economic and social systems*. What distinguishes ACCESS is that it is a federal-provincial and, in places, an interprovincial approach to securing the socio-economic union. This represents a sharp break from our post-war tradition where Ottawa was both the standard-setter and enforcer of the internal common market. But in light of the set of forces detailed above, we really have no choice but to forge a federal-provincial partnership and in some cases an interprovincial accord in order to deliver an effective internal union. In terms of coverage, however, the components of ACCESS are rather straightforward — the economic union, the social union, labour market integration, reworking fiscal federalism and approaches relating to accommodating the increasing policy interdependencies between the two levels of government. Some of these areas and proposals are lifted directly from the recent *Report to Premiers* by the Ministerial Council On Social Policy Reform and Renewal (1995). Others are adapted from my previous work (Courchene, 1994) and the writings of other policy analysts (e.g., Burelle, 1995, 1996). While detail will be provided later, this brief overview of the range of issues subsumed under ACCESS is probably adequate for introductory purposes.

In more detail, the analysis proceeds as follows. Part II focusses on a set of framework axioms or precepts that ought to subtend any federal-provincial agreement on the socio-economic union. While many of these are rather uncontroversial (e.g., transparency), some do touch upon substantive issues (e.g., the principle of subsidiarity).

Part III then addresses the substantive elements of a Canadian Convention on the socio-economic union. The analysis develops two models. The first of these is referred to as an "interim" model — it maintains many of the features of the status quo, it is federal-provincial in nature and it is broadly consistent with recent pronouncements of both levels of government. The second or "steady-state" model is more consistent with the scenario outlined in the introduction to this paper — it involves substantial alteration of the status quo, it is more interprovincial in nature and it embodies considerable disentanglement and decentralization. While, as noted, the latter is more consistent with the foregoing analysis, it may well be that the interim model is a necessary half-way house on the road to the more thoroughgoing approach to a reworked socio-economic union. For both of these variants, the analysis will attempt to grapple with the design of acceptable common-market principles. However, these principles will lack full detail because they will inevitably be derived from intense federal-provincial or interprovincial negotiation.

In Part IV, the analysis turns to the issues of enforcement and remedies. Are there ways to make ACCESS binding on all governments and, if so, how? Not surprisingly, this will be a more difficult issue for the steady-state or full-blown version of ACCESS. Part V then addresses some process issues, followed by a brief concluding section.

There is one other aspect of ACCESS that merits highlight in this introduction. Running throughout the analysis will be the recognition that a Convention on the socio-economic union, while of necessity an agreement among governments, is first and foremost about the rights and privileges of citizens, consumers, labour and enterprise on the socio-economic front. This is the rationale for the acronym ACCESS.

Prior to directing attention to these three core areas — framework axioms, pan-Canadian common-market principles and enforcement/remedies issues — it is instructive to address a key operating assumption of ACCESS, namely that an effective internal socio-economic union must require the combined efforts of all levels of government.

The Provincial Imperative

Securing the socio-economic union in post-war Canada was essentially left to Ottawa. And Ottawa rose to the challenge, largely by creative use of the spending power. On the taxation front, for example, the tax collection agreements for the personal income tax have become a model for federal nations — decentralized yet substantially harmonized. Ottawa stands ready to collect provincial taxes, largely free of charge, as long as the provinces adhere to a set of non-discriminatory provisions. (Admittedly, this statement excludes Quebec which has its own personal income tax, but this province has signed on to other tax harmonization measures.) On the social policy front, the use of shared-cost programs and other initiatives have allowed Canada to convert the various provincial programs into "national" ones by guaranteeing principles such as portability for health care and, for welfare, the absence of residency requirements. In the language of the Charlottetown Accord, this is "negative integration", namely a series of top-down "thou shalt nots" — thou shalt not extra bill, thou shalt not impose residency requirements, etc. While this is important and remains important, it is no longer sufficient. What is increasingly required is "positive integration" — a pro-active meshing of provincial systems (skills transferability) and federal-provincial systems (consumption tax harmonization). This cannot be done without the full participation of the provinces. Hence, delivering a full-blown socio-economic union requires both top-down (vertical) and bottom-up (horizontal) integration.

That this is the case is becoming progressively more evident. As more powers are passed down (back?) to the provinces, as indicated in the Speech from the Throne, provincial involvement becomes ever-more essential. Moreover, as Ottawa pares cash transfers to the provinces under the CHST, from roughly $18 billion this year to the announced floor of $11 billion at the turn of the century, it is losing both its moral authority and its financial capability for enforcing unilateral top-down standards. In terms of the latter (financial enforcement), it is interesting to note that a provincial sales tax at roughly half the average provincial rate would give Alberta more money than it will get in federal transfers at the turn of the century. Indeed, Alberta's current budget surplus exceeds the amount of federal transfers to the province. This highlights the federal dilemma and explains in part why the 1995 federal budget called for the development of a set of "mutual consent" principles to underpin the CHST. Beyond these financial considerations, the increasing north-south nature of the Canadian economy in tandem with the quite distinct provincial economies will imply different approaches on the part of the various provinces in terms of designing and delivering their respective social envelopes. In turn this means that any notion of identical standards across all provinces is a non-starter — much of the negotiation will have to be in terms of principles and "equivalencies". Finally, the need for involving the provinces was explicitly recognized by Ottawa in its last two budgets as well as in the Throne Speech. Basically, this amounts to a federal recognition that the existing principles (e.g., the five Canada Health Act principles and the prohibition of residency requirements for welfare) can no longer deliver the needed degree of integration in terms of the internal socio-economic union. In large measure, the march of globalization and the knowledge/information revolution require new approaches to preserving and promoting the Canadian common market. And key to any and all of these new approaches is a partnership among the various orders of government in Canada.

There is another perspective that can be brought to bear on all of this. In order to create and integrate our "national" social policy network in the 50s and 60s, Ottawa needed to play an overarching role. And central to this role were the development of the various shared-cost programs and the evolution of our comprehensive equalization program. As these social programs matured and became "established", it was only natural to shift funding from a conditional (shared-cost) basis to unconditional grants. Now that social Canada is in need of restructuring in the face of a variety of forces (economic, fiscal, demographic, etc.), the roles of the two orders of government in this renewed process are now radically altered. Specifically, apart from providing certain social services to First Nations, Ottawa is not really a player in the social policy design and delivery game. It has no option except to leave this to the provinces. Thus, while transfers, subsidies, principles, fines and the like were appropriate in terms of initially creating our social network, these instruments are ill-suited in terms of forging the needed national or interprovincial integration of this "second-round" of social program design. This would be true even if there were no cuts and caps and freezes to federal-provincial transfers. The provinces must rise to the citizen and societal challenge by accepting a larger responsibility for preserving and promoting social Canada.

Thus, bringing in the provinces should not be construed as in any way a watering down of the internal socio-economic union. Quite the opposite. Indeed, part of the reason why the German and Swiss and Australian federations have more thoroughgoing integration in terms of transferability of skills, for example, is that Canada has never attempted to bring the provinces meaningfully into the operational workings of our internal union. Canadians deserve better and this can only come from a partnership approach to our east-west internal union.

This being said, however, there are differing degrees of provincial (and federal) involvement. The "interim" model of the Convention calls for federal-provincial cooperation and co-determination in terms of securing the economic union, whereas the steady-state or full ACCESS model assumes a greater role for interprovincial management of the internal union, in line with existing constitutional responsibilities especially in the social policy areas.

II: FRAMEWORK AXIOMS

In designing a convention on the socio-economic union there are certain underlying axioms or principles that should apply irrespective of the content of any such convention. Indeed, most of the following axioms ought to apply to any policy area. Among these general framework axioms are the following:

• FA#1: Accountability

Governments must be accountable to citizens for the prudent use of public monies and the programs that incorporate these funds. In the current Canadian context, enhanced accountability means a clarifying of the roles of the two levels of government in the social sphere. A useful companion to accountability is the *principle of fiscal coincidence:* the jurisdiction responsible for spending funds should in general be the one responsible for raising them in the first place. The existence of intergovernmental transfers is an obvious exception to this principle, an exception that can be rationalized in a variety of ways (e.g., economies of scale in raising taxes). However, in these circumstances, the design of the transfer system should be as consistent as possible in terms of isolating the locus of responsibility and, therefore, accountability.

• FA#2: Transparency

This principle is closely related to accountability. If programs are not transparent, accountability will become blurred. The existing CHST transfer system, with its combination of cash transfers and tax point transfers, is hopelessly complex and, therefore, at cross purposes with any transparency principle. In the recent past, Ottawa has been able to claim that transfers (cash plus tax points) to the provinces have increased while the provinces have argued that federal transfers (cash transfers, since this is all that is really transferred) have fallen. And both parties can substantiate their claims. As a result, citizens become confused and accountability becomes diffused. In any new convention, the provisions must be transparent so that all parties (including citizens) recognize where accountability resides.

• FA#3: Efficiency

Given the fiscal burden at all levels of government, efficiency becomes a virtue. Beyond the obvious, namely ensuring that no more than the essential amounts of funds are expended in terms of achieving a particular policy goal, there are other facets to efficiency. One is the appropriate matching of policy instruments to policy objectives: if the objective is distributional, then it should be delivered via a distributional instrument (e.g., the tax-transfer system), not via an allocative instrument. Another is that where intergovernmental transfers are involved, the incentives should not be such as to encourage what elsewhere (Courchene, 1994) I have labelled "intergovernmental gaming" (for example, the incentives under existing legislation for provincial governments to create make-work projects to transfer citizens from provincial welfare to federal UI). Finally, the elimination of duplication and overlap has an obvious efficiency component and in the process it probably also contributes to enhanced transparency and accountability.

• FA#4: Equity

In the context of reconstituting the social and economic union there are at least two types of equity issues that must be addressed. The first is that we must respect the *equalization principle* — all provinces must have ACCESS to revenues sufficient to ensure that they can provide reasonably comparable public services at reasonably comparable tax rates (s.36(2) of the *Constitution Act, 1982)*. The second is *fiscal neutrality*. This is the proposition that, apart from equalization, federal programs should treat similarly situated individuals equally, regardless of place of residence. The existing UI provisions fall way short of this mark: an unemployed individual in New Brunswick is more than twice as likely to be in receipt of UI benefits as a similarly situated Ontarian (Courchene, 1994 and Sargent, 1995). In many cases, federal transfers other than those for equalization ought to treat provinces equally on a per capita basis. These two equity principles are related in the sense that if equal-per-capita transfers for the CHST, for example, serve to undermine the equalization principle, then the latter should be adjusted appropriately. Violation of either of these principles will severely undermine the likelihood of achieving a thorough convention on the socio-economic union. More ominously, the federal proclivity for introducing an equalization element in every federal program will almost certainly serve to undermine support for the formal equalization program. This would spell the end of social Canada!

• FA#5: Citizen Rights

While the Convention will be an intergovernmental agreement, the underlying rationale is to provide basic rights and privileges for all Canadians. Hence, the presumption associated with the specific details of any provisions of an internal socio-economic union should always be on the side of citizens. In other words, the burden of proof in terms of defending any derogations from the Convention must reside with governments, not with citizens. The specific ways in which this principle can become operational will be dealt with in the appropriate later context.

While ACCESS is a goal in its own right, it is also the case that it is a key ingredient in the larger on-going context of proposals to revitalize and rebalance the federation, e.g., the report of the Group of 22 (1996). Hence, as a bridge between the above framework axioms and the later common-market principles, there are several rebalancing and revitalization precepts that merit highlight.

• FA#6: The Principle of Subsidiarity

The principle of subsidiarity states that government should be as close as possible to citizens: powers or competences should be delegated to the lowest level of government where they can be effectively exercised. This implies a bias toward decentralization. However, if the nature of the service or the activity means that it cannot be carried out efficiently at the local level, then a higher level of government should assume responsibility. The presence of cross-provincial policy spillovers, for example, would imply the need for an upward shift of the policy area. But upward need not mean central: it could also mean interprovincial or federal-provincial.

• FA#7: The Federal Principle

Subject to adhering to the provisions of the Convention, the provinces must have the flexibility to design and deliver their own vision and version of the socio-economic envelope. Economists typically refer to this as competitive federalism. The most cited exemplar here is the experimentation in Saskatchewan which led to Medicare. Recently, this province has substituted free drugs to the elderly with a system based on ability to pay. Other provinces are following suit. The more general point is that the on-going blossoming of provincial experimentation across a range of fronts is absolutely critical to recreating an efficient and viable social Canada. The policy challenge here is to ensure that this experimentation takes place within a framework of "national" (federal, federal-provincial or interprovincial) norms or principles.

• FA#8: The Spending Power Provision (Federal Flexibility)

Corresponding to this provincial flexibility, there is a need to retain federal flexibility as well. Specifically, the federal government should be able to exercise its spending power in areas of provincial jurisdiction provided that the provinces can opt out with compensation. Whether this opting out must relate to the establishment of an equivalent program (as in the Throne Speech) or whether opting out should be unconditional (as in the report of the Group of 22) is obviously an issue of some contention, but some version of the spending power provision is important to ensure federal flexibility.

• FA#9: Uniform Application (Equal Partners)

Newfoundland, as part of the *Constitution Act, 1982,* has the right to discriminate in hiring in favour of its residents. Likewise, the federal government, under s.36(1) of the Constitution, has the responsibility for "promoting equal opportunities for the well-being of Canadians" and for "furthering economic development to reduce disparity in opportunities". However, ACCESS should have uniform applicability on all signatories. There should be no derogations from citizens rights to the social and economic union. There are several reasons for this. First, the Convention will be a symbol of who and what we are as a federation. Accordingly, this should be a statement of uniform rights for citizens across the country. Second, the Convention will be an intergovernmental agreement, not part of the Constitution. Hence, the Constitution will trump the Convention. This being the case, there is no need for derogations in the Convention. Third, the existence of derogations will likely torpedo the Convention. The notion that Ottawa could, as part of the Convention, discriminate against Ontario on regional equity grounds while Ontario could not, again as part of the Convention, react to this discrimination will surely mean that the Convention will never see the light of day. In practical terms, what this means is that the onus is on Ottawa to be willing to enter the Convention on equal terms with the provinces and on the provinces to ensure that they are also equally and severally bound.

• FA#10: Duality and Asymmetry

While uniform application, as in the previous framework axiom, is imperative, this need not mean that the end result will be symmetrical for all provinces. For example, some provinces may wish to impose standards higher than those embodied in the Convention. As long as these are non-discriminatory in nature, this should be encouraged even if the result will be asymmetrical. Similarly, to the extent that Quebec may be more likely than other provinces to draw down all powers offered, this, too, should pose no problem. Phrased differently, the design of the Convention should respect the *duality* aspect of our federation (i.e., two languages of convergence). Asymmetries can also arise from transfers of powers upward. For example, if not all provinces are in favour of transferring responsibility for securities regulation to the federal government, this should not stand in the way of those that wish to do so. Our federation is already highly asymmetrical. Contrary to much received opinion, these asymmetries are best viewed as solutions rather than problems. For example, the fact that Quebec has its own personal income tax (an asymmetrical feature) means that the rest of the provinces can achieve a much higher degree of harmonization than otherwise would be the case in terms of the joint federal-provincial, personal-income-tax arrangements. Finally, it is important to recognise that the asymmetries that may arise in the Convention are *de facto* asymmetries, not *de jure* asymmetries.

• FA#11: Provincial Treatment

The principle of "provincial treatment" must be the core operating principle in any Convention on the socio-economic union. This is the internal union counterpart of "national treatment" under the FTA. In terms of the latter, Canada has considerable freedom to design its own policies, provided only that they do not discriminate between Canadians and Americans. Transferred to the Convention, provincial treatment means that New Brunswick, for example, can design its internal policies as it wishes, provided a) that in their implementation New Brunswick does not discriminate in favour of its own residents and b) that they abide by other provisions of the Convention. Others may wish to refer to this as the "principle of non-discrimination".

• FA#12: Standstill Provisions

The Convention will not likely deliver an unimpeded internal socio-economic union. Certainly, the status quo falls way short of the mark here. Hence, the goal should be to improve on the status quo — to aim to free up the socio-economic union in selected areas and to prevent "slippage" in all other areas. This is the concept of *standstill*, namely to ensure that there is no backtracking in terms of existing common-market achievements. Adherence to this principle will guarantee that the Convention will be an improvement on the interprovincial or pan-Canadian aspects of the status quo.[1]

With no claim to being exhaustive, these framework principles provide a launchpad for designing a new Convention on the Canadian social and economic union. We now turn to an analysis of the substance and principles that this Convention might contain.

III: ACCESS: PAN-CANADIAN PRINCIPLES FOR THE SOCIO-ECONOMIC UNION

The above framework principles are consistent with a variety of approaches to a Canadian Convention on the internal union. Our principal interest in this section is elaborating upon the full-blown model that takes the framework principles to their logical and Constitutional limit. Not surprisingly, this will be referred to as the "full" ACCESS model. However, the model cannot be implemented tomorrow since, as will become apparent, the variant proposed below calls for interprovincial accords with respect to labour market and social union issues, the conversion of cash transfers into tax-point transfers, a series of federal-provincial administrative amendments and a set of dispute-resolutions procedures and enforcement mechanisms for securing the internal union. Hence, the negotiation process will involve healthy doses of both time and goodwill.

This being the case, the stage is set for the implementation of what will be referred to as the "interim" ACCESS model, which *can* be implemented tomorrow. The basic feature of this interim model is that it is broadly consistent with the series of recent "official" pronouncements by both levels of government on the evolution of the social union, e.g., the last two federal budgets and the Speech from the Throne on Ottawa's part and the *Report to Premiers* (1995) on the provinces' part. These two models are consistent with each other in the sense that the interim model is probably an essential stepping stone and building block toward the full ACCESS model.

In order to breathe some reality into this discussion, Table 1 represents a workable prototype of an interim model while Table 2 is my own proposal for what a full-blown ACCESS model might look like. While the lines of demarcation between these two approaches are no doubt blurred in places, the following key differences are evident:

- The interim model is more federal and federal-provincial in nature whereas the full ACCESS model is more federal-provincial and interprovincial. In other words, the full ACCESS model is more consistent with the provisions of the Constitution in vesting responsibility for areas like social policy and labour-market training with the provinces.

- The federal-provincial financial interface differs significantly between the two models. The interim model contemplates the continuation of federal cash transfers with the important proviso that they will be monitored by a federal-provincial mechanism rather than by the current federal enforcement. On the other hand, the full ACCESS model requires the conversion of the cash transfers into equalized tax-point transfers, along the lines of the fiscal coincidence provision under FA#1 above.

TABLE 1: A Prototype of the Interim ACCESS Model

Social Union

- Essentially the status quo prevails;
- The five *Canada Health Act* principles would remain, as would the prohibition of residency requirements for welfare;
- The $11 billion cash transfer floor (as per the 1996 federal budget) would obtain;
- Financial penalties (reductions in cash transfers) would continue for violation of social union principles. However, the monitoring of these penalties would fall to a federal-provincial oversight agency rather than the current federal oversight.

Division of Powers

- Training would be devolved to the provinces;
- So would tourism, mining, recreation, etc., as indicated in the Throne Speech;
- The federal spending power would be circumscribed, again as outlined in the Throne Speech;
- Ottawa would accommodate an upward transfer of powers (e.g., securities regulation) for those provinces willing to do so;
- The end result may well involve asymmetry.

Economic Union

- Commitment to both orders of government to fully implement the *Agreement on Internal Trade*.

Coordination

- The powers of the Secretariat (as required under the AIT) would expand to monitor these arrangements;
- There would need to be an appeal process and a dispute-resolution mechanism, replete with decision rules for the parties.

Prospect

- While this is a modest alteration of the evolving status quo, it might develop into an European-style co-determination model with respect to a broad range of economic, social and policy interdependency issues.

TABLE 2: A Prototype of the Full ACCESS Model

Social Union

- Full provincial responsibility for design and delivery of health, social services and education in line with the principles in the *Report to Premiers*.
- Enforceable interprovincial accord whereby the provinces jointly implement and maintain a framework of principles and standards/equivalencies that will guarantee across Canada rights such as mobility and portability.

Fiscal Relations

- An effective equalization program guaranteeing all provinces the ability to provide reasonably comparable public services at reasonably comparable tax rates.
- Beyond equalization, fiscal neutrality would obtain (FA#4).
- Conversion of existing federal cash transfers into equalized tax-point transfers.
- Allow provinces to levy a "tax on base" (as an alternative to the current "tax on tax") under the shared personal-income-tax system.

Labour Markets

- Full provincial responsibility for all labour market development measures.
- Federal-provincial co-management of UI (along with greater accountability to employers and employees who now fully finance the system) so it can be integrated into provincial designs for overall human capital policy. As an alternative, one could provincialize UI (via equalization of UI premium income).
- Interprovincial agreement on mutual recognition of training and qualifications across provinces.

Economic Union

- Incorporate an expanded s.121 (into ACCESS) to include labour, capital and services. Consider enshrining this in the Constitution, at some future date.
- A commitment by all parties to remove all internal barriers to trade with a specified time period (i.e., to implement fully the provisions of the 1994 Agreement on Internal Trade).

Coordination & Flexibility

- Embrace subsidiarity, allowing powers to be transferred down (e.g., forestry, mining, recreation, etc. as in the Throne Speech) and upward or horizontally (e.g., national securities commission, national tax agency etc.).
- Ensure policy flexibility by accepting FA#7 and FA#8 above;
- Incorporate initiatives designed to manage policy interdependencies among governments, e.g., "reciprocal federalism" as elaborated in the text.

- The enforcement/remedies also differ dramatically. The interim model is a variant of the status quo, with the above-noted difference that the financial transfers will now be overseen by a federal-provincial body. Since there are no cash transfers (except for equalization) under full model, this places a premium on designing mechanisms to ensure that the Convention is binding on the parties.

In terms of proceeding, it is convenient initially to devote brief attention to spelling out how the interim model might work. This will facilitate the more in-depth analysis of the full-blown ACCESS model.

A: A Workable Interim Model

At one level, implementing an interim model of the type reflected in Table 1 is rather straightforward:

- On the social side, the five CHA principles would be maintained, as would the prohibition of residency requirements for welfare.

- On the labour market side, Ottawa would follow through with its Throne Speech commitments to devolve labour-market training to the provinces and to circumscribe the exercise of the federal spending power (along the lines of FA#8 above).

- The interim accord could involve processes to manage the policy interdependencies between the two levels of government (but this would probably best be left for the full model). However, it should involve commitments to reinforce the economic union, probably via best efforts measures to deliver on various provisions of the *Agreement On Internal Trade (1994)*.

- Monitoring would be done by a federal-provincial agency (or group of ministers) that would report to the First Ministers.

- Citizen or government challenges to this accord would first go to a panel of experts for adjudication. If sustained, the remedies could vary, but would include the withholding of cash transfers by the federal-provincial monitoring body.

- The accord would be signed for successive five-year periods.

These provisions track fairly closely the provisions contained in Table 1. More importantly, they resonate well with existing proposals from both levels of government. This is by design since one of the criteria of this interim accord is that it be implementable immediately. To be sure, others may have structured the accord somewhat differently, but this is inevitable in this sort of exercise.

Among the several potential problems with this type (and likely any type) of interim accord, two in particular merit highlight since they lead directly to the sorts of provisions embodied in the later full-blown ACCESS model. The first is that this sort of accord is not likely to bind the federal government. It is true that the existing federal unilateralism in assessing whether a province is in violation of the common-market principles would be replaced, under the interim model, by federal-provincial monitoring and oversight. While the voting mechanism was not spelled out, one could imagine, for example, that if either the provinces (at least 7 provinces with 50% of the population) or Ottawa supports the decision of the expert panel, then the panel's decision will hold. However, the real issue arises with the level of cash transfers. Given the Supreme Court decision on the Canada Assistance Plan challenge (to be detailed later), it is not at all obvious that this sort of interim accord could guarantee the $11 billion CHST cash transfer floor after the turn of the century (as outlined in the 1996 federal budget). In other words, the federal government would still be free, constitutionally, to repeat the series of unilateral series of cuts, freezes and caps to cash transfers that occurred over the last decade and that are still in progress. The full ACCESS model attempts to address this issue by means that include, among other approaches, parallel legislation passed by all governments. To be sure, these approaches could be incorporated into an interim accord, but since the negotiations pursuant to this would likely be intense, not to mention time-consuming, much of the value of an interim (i.e., immediate) model would fall by the wayside. Why not go directly to the full-blown ACCESS variant?

The second area is equally problematic: the social policy area is in full evolution, so much so that relying on the five CHA principles is likely to do more harm than good. The *Report to Premiers* expressed the issue rather well:

> Premiers have indicated their unanimous support for a publicly funded health system and are committed to the *Canada Health Act* as one dimension of the system. However, the Canadian health system has evolved beyond physician and hospital care, and includes a wide range of preventative, promotive, supportive and rehabilitative services. As well, it has become widely recognized that a whole range of factors outside the health system are important determinants of health. The *Canada Health Act* narrowly focusses on insured physician and hospital services, and does not recognize the extent to which the health system has evolved.(1995, p. 11)

But even this is too narrow a vision of health. Progressively, the system is evolving toward a conception of *well-being*, not just old-style health care. What Canada probably needs is a pan-Canadian *Well-Being Act* replete with its own set of principles relating to portability, public administration, comprehensiveness, ACCESS and universality. It is likely that under this system coverage will be enhanced (i.e., become more comprehensive), portability and universality will be guaranteed, but ACCESS will become subject to ability-to-pay user fees, most likely delayed and reconciled through the personal tax system. In other words the system will become more European in nature — extended coverage but with some role for ability-to-pay private financing throughout the system.

The essential point here is not to attempt to guesstimate the likely evolution of the health or well-being sector, but rather to emphasize that the driving factors underpinning this evolution are the efficiency, equity and fiscal concerns triggered in part by the massive cuts to cash transfers under the CHST, which are only now beginning to bite. In effect the CHST is in the process of transforming the design and delivery of both health and welfare. In a real sense, there is no status quo in these areas. The longer term solution probably requires a combination of a) an explicit recognition on the part of Ottawa that its actions are generating a new era in terms of health and welfare, b) an assurance from the provinces that they will not back off their impressive set of social policy principles incorporated in the *Report to Premiers* (and reproduced as Table 3), and c) a negotiation of a new social contract among the provinces, Ottawa and selected stakeholders. But, this, too, is really much more in line with the full ACCESS model than with the interim variant.

Despite these potential problems, the concept of an interim model has much to recommend it, since there is a need to establish a new, temporary, status quo while negotiations with respect to the full ACCESS model are on-going. Most of the pieces for this interim model are either already in place or can be with the stroke of a pen. Thus, there is no reason why it could not be fully operative by year's end. If this does not come to pass, the recent conflicts with Alberta over health and with British Columbia over welfare will begin to multiply, and not only in the "have" provinces.

But this is diverting attention away from the core thrust of the paper — to outline a Canadian Convention on the socio-economic union consistent with the emerging globalization and knowledge/information paradigms, with the framework axioms of section II and with the letter and spirit of the Constitution. To this I now turn.

B: The Full ACCESS Model

Most of the key elements in a full-blown version of ACCESS appear in Table 2. Even a cursory glance at these provisions indicate that this is a highly decentralized

TABLE 3: Principles to Guide Social Policy Reform and Renewal

Social Programs Must Be Accessible and Serve the Basic Needs of All Canadians

1. Social policy must assure reasonable access to health, education and training, income support and social services that meet Canadians' basic needs.

2. Social policy must support and protect Canadians most in need.

3. Social policy must promote social and economic conditions which enhance self-sufficiency and well-being, to assist all Canadians to actively participate in economic and social life.

4. Social policy must promote active development of an individuals' skills and capabilities as the foundation for social and economic development.

5. Social policy must promote the well-being of children and families, as children are our future. It must ensure the protection and development of children and youth in a health, safe and nurturing environment.

Social Programs Must Reflect Our Individual and Collective Responsibility

6. Social policy must reflect our individual and collective responsibility for health, education and social security, and reinforce the commitment of Canadians to the dignity and independence of the individual.

7. Partnerships among governments, communities, social organizations, business, labour, families and individuals are essential to the continued strength of our social system.

8. There is a continuing and important role, to be defined, for both orders of government in the establishment, maintenance and interpretation of national principles for social programs.

Social Programs Must be Affordable, Effective and Accountable

9. The ability to fund social programs must be protected. Social programs must be affordable, sustainable, and designed to achieve intended and measurable results.

10. The long-term benefits of prevention and early intervention must be reflected in the design of social programs.

11. Federal constitutional, fiduciary, treaty and other historic responsibilities for assurance of Aboriginal health, income support, social services, housing, training and educational opportunities must be fulfilled. The federal government must recognize its financial responsibilities for Aboriginal Canadians, both on and off reserve.

12. Governments must coordinate and integrate social programming and funding in order to ensure efficient and effective program delivery, and to reduce waste and duplication.

... continued

TABLE 3 (cont'd.)

Social Programs Must be Flexible, Responsive and Reasonably Comparable Across Canada

13. Social policy must be flexible and responsive to changing social and economic conditions, regional/local priorities and individual circumstances.

14. Governments must ensure that all Canadians have access to reasonably comparable basic social programming throughout Canada, and ensure that Canadians are treated with fairness and equity.

15. Social policy must recognize and take into account the differential impact social programming can have on men and women.

Source: *Report to Premiers (op. cit.).*

approach to securing the internal common market, with any attendant externalities/ spillovers to be sorted out largely via interprovincial accords rather than federal intervention. However, it is also evident that the only way in which Ottawa could possibly consent to several of these provisions is if the interprovincial mechanisms for securing the internal union are binding on all parties and in particular on the provinces. As already noted, this puts a premium on issues relating to compliance, enforcement and remedies. These critical issues are the subject of part IV. The role of the present section is to elaborate on the substance of a full-blown ACCESS, drawing heavily from Table 2. In so doing, I shall deal with the social and fiscal categories together since they are closely related. Then, in turn, attention will be directed to the labour market, to the economic union and, finally, to the coordination of the policy interdependencies between the two levels of government.

1: Promoting and Financing the Social Union

As Table 2 indicates, full responsibility for the design and delivery of health, welfare and education would devolve to the provinces.[2] This is the "closer to the people" component of subsidiarity (FA#6). The externalities or pan-Canadian components of subsidiarity would be addressed via an interprovincial accord which would embody principles and standards as well as measures to guarantee mobility and portability. On the fiscal side, the proposal incorporates both the equalization and the fiscal neutrality principles (FA#4). More significantly, the interprovincial accord presumes a complete federal withdrawal from the area since cash transfers would be transferred into additional equalized tax-point transfers.

By way of elaboration of the last element (additional tax-point transfers), this would certainly remove the concern of the interim model where the federal government might continue with the on-going process of reducing cash transfers: these would now be provincial revenues. It is also worth noting that transferring additional tax points to the provinces would serve to bring the rest of the provinces in rough alignment with the existing treatment of Quebec, which is currently in receipt of an additional 16.5 personal income tax (PIT) points. Finally, with the enhanced decentralization in the social policy area (as well as the labour market area), greater provincial participation in the income tax system makes eminent sense since this will increasingly be the vehicle of choice in terms of delivering and integrating much of the social envelope and probably the labour-market envelope as well. In order to facilitate this flexibility, Table 2 recommends that provinces be able to levy their portion of the shared personal-income-tax system on the federally determined base for taxable income, rather than the current system which limits the provinces to taxing federal tax payable. In the jargon of the tax-collection arrangements, this proposal is usually referred to as a "tax on base". (For more details, see Ontario Economic Council, 1983 and Courchene, 1994).

Given that the federal government is on record as being against further PIT tax-point transfers, the only possible way that this can become a reality in ACCESS is for the provinces to demonstrate to themselves, to the federal government and, most of all, to Canadians that they indeed have the will and the ability to design and deliver an effective internal social union Convention. The key building blocks required for this exercise are fairly obvious. For example, the Table 2 commitment to guarantees with respect to portability and mobility are clearly essential. And the Table 3 social policy principles would be shared by the vast majority of Canadians. The challenge then becomes one of integrating these guarantees and principles in a manner that generates a set of operational pan-Canadian norms or standards or equivalencies. Perhaps these could be accompanied by a set of minimum standards for specific areas. (As an aside, it is interesting to note that there never have been minimum standards for welfare benefits under CAP, for example). This exercise will hardly be easy, particularly since both health and welfare policy areas are in full evolutionary flight, but the goal is achievable. Indeed, it must be achievable since a pan-Canadian social safety is a core Canadian value. And, increasingly, it is only with support of the provinces that Canada can fully deliver on this goal. That this basic message has not been filtered down to citizens constitutes a major stumbling block. With its call for mutual-consent principles in the 1995 budget (and reiterated in the 1996 budget and the Throne Speech), Ottawa has reconciled itself to this reality. It now needs to communicate this to Canadians.

2: UI/Labour Markets

With the advent of the CHST, the Throne Speech commitment to transfer labour-market training to the provinces, and the more recent promise to devolve the "developmental" aspects of UI (now EI) to the provinces, the obvious and logical next step is to ensure that UI itself is more integrated into the provincial (or regional) social policy systems. What is essential is that the constellation of programs coming within the UI/training/education/welfare subsystem be forged into an integrated whole. This is the human-capital imperative, expressed so forcefully by Lester Thurow (1993): "If capital is borrowable, raw materials are buyable and technology is copyable, what are you left with if you want to run a high-wage economy? Only skills, there isn't anything else". Since the federal government, with the CHST and the devolution of training, has apparently abandoned any attempt or desire to forge this integration, it has to fall to the provinces. This is even more evident with the recent announcement by Human Resources Minister Doug Young that for those interested in job creation, "knock on the door of your provincial legislature" (Greenspon, 1996). Table 2 speaks in terms of co-determination of UI among the provinces, Ottawa, labour and management. It also specifies an obvious and more disentangled alternative, which would be to "provincialize" UI, with the proviso that the UI premium income be equalized to ensure that all provinces have at least the five-province average of premium income per capita. (Courchene, 1994, 283).

With either the provincialized version of UI or the federal-provincial version in place, the *quid quo pro* on the provincial front would have to be an interprovincial mutual recognition of skills accreditation and certification so that training becomes fully mobile across provincial boundaries. An important step in this direction is the mutual recognition provisions (chapter 7) of the *Agreement on Internal Trade* (AIT), with even more recent support for mutual recognition of training embodied on the *Report To Premiers* (1995,16). While this commitment to mutual recognition could be subsumed in the economic union section of Table 2, it is important for substantive as well as symbolic reasons that it become part and parcel of the UI/labour market provisions of ACCESS.

3: The Economic Union

The economic union provisions of Table 2 represent, as they must in any full-blown ACCESS model, a significant improvement on the status quo in terms of freeing up the flow of goods, services, capital and labour within Canada. As already noted, all governments initialled the AIT in 1994. However, as detailed in the excellent C.D. Howe volume on the AIT (*Getting There...*,1995), too many of the key provisions are in the nature of best-efforts intentions to removing existing barriers. Thus, the firm commitment to remove all existing barriers with a reasonable time frame, as proposed in Table 2, would be most appropriate and most welcome.

With these measures in place and agreed to, it becomes rather natural to include in ACCESS an enlarged s.121 of the Constitution. Section 121 currently reads as follows:

> All articles of the Growth, Produce, or Manufacture of any one of the Provinces shall, from and after the Union, be admitted free into each of the other Provinces.

While it is likely that, in light of the FTA and NAFTA, the courts will begin to interpret s.121 more expansively, the fact of the matter is that, as written, this provision does not refer to labour, services or capital. It must. A stronger commitment to provisions guaranteeing the economic union is a *sine qua non* for enhanced decentralization and is an essential ingredient of the full ACCESS model. In accordance with FA#9 (uniform application), this should be a straightforward provision equally applicable to all governments (i.e., no derogations written into the provision). While Table 2 runs in terms of incorporating an expanded version of s.121 as part of the Convention, the ideal solution would be to enshrine this in the Constitution.

4: Coordination and Flexibility

The final panel of Table 2 focusses on issues relating to coordination and flexibility. The first two entries attempt to ensure that the Convention is consistent with the rebalancing and revitalization of the federation. Hence the emphasis on the principle of subsidiarity, as well as the acceptance of competitive federalism and the role of the federal spending power. It may well be that the result of these measures will imply greater asymmetry across provinces. For example, some provinces may not want to take up the Throne Speech offer to devolve forestry, mining, recreation, etc. And not all provinces might be willing to follow Ontario's 1996 budget proposal to transfer securities regulation upwards.

The remainder of this panel addresses, in skeletal form, the challenge of increasing policy interdependencies among governments. Admittedly, one of the roles of the social/labour-market accords is to accommodate and internalize horizontal (cross-provincial) policy spillovers. However, the issue addressed here relates more to vertical or federal-provincial harmonization.

In a recent article, Richard Zuker (1995) focusses on this very issue. He argues that because of the demise of the federal spending power and because of the on-going decentralization, new arrangements are required to minimize the potential negative spillovers arising from vertical policy interdependencies. Zuker refers to these potential arrangements as "reciprocal federalism". The name is particularly apt since the concept recognizes, at base, that the provinces need Ottawa to act in certain ways in order that *provincial* policies become more effective. Similarly, Ottawa needs some help from the provinces in order that *federal* policies be more effective. No matter what label one places on such arrangements, it is obvious that there exist plenty of opportunities for mutual gain arising from enhanced coordination, harmonization or even just from greater information sharing.

The challenge is probably most acute in the macroeconomic area. Debt and deficits, for example, are a national concern not just a federal concern. And appropriate stabilization policy cannot ignore the fact the provinces (with the municipalities) now spend more than Ottawa does. For example, Ontario's policy in the late 1980s was way offside with overall macro policy and particularly monetary policy. By revving up expenditures to the mid-teens in the context of an already overheated provincial economy, Ontario's actions forced the Bank of Canada, in its pursuit of price stability, to raise interest rates (and, hence, the value of the dollar) to levels that would not otherwise have been called for. In the event, Ontario paid dearly for this, since the combination of high interest and exchange rates exacted an enormous economic toll on Ontario in the early-1990s recession. The point here is not to attempt to assign blame. Rather, it is to make the important observation that incompatible policies can exact high penalties on everybody. Hence, mechanisms that allow for information-sharing at a minimum and perhaps some formal coordination are warranted.

Toward this end, ACCESS should provide a framework for this to occur. One approach is to follow the Australian example, where there is a pre-budget-cycle First Ministers' Conference which makes public the projected expenditures, revenues and deficits of all governments on a consistent accounting basis. These forecasts assume no change in any fiscal parameters and they present the data for two income-growth scenarios. It is surprising that there is no counterpart to this in Canada. Because the business cycles across the provinces and regions do not move in synch, it is not obvious that any formal attempt at full harmonization of macro policy is appropriate, but what surely is appropriate as a first step is the greater information-sharing and transparency that would follow from adopting the Australian approach. This is an area where "learning by doing" is probably the appropriate strategy.

Another example of potential policy coordination relates to the challenge arising from federal government participation in international treaties that touch upon areas of exclusive provincial jurisdiction. Again Australia provides a useful comparison with their recent proposal for a "Treaties Council" as part of their equivalent of our First Ministers' Conference. The German federation has taken this even further. In the context of the European Union, if an issue is up for discussion that falls under the constitutional responsibility of the lander (i.e., provinces), then lander representatives (i.e., the upper chamber or Bundesrat, since it is what Canadians might call a "House of the Provinces") will take the lead in negotiations (Courchene 1996a). The point here is not to argue for "importing" institutional procedures from other federations. Rather, it is to suggest a full-blown ACCESS model has the potential for evolving into a co-determination model in the treaties area, so that Canada can speak with one voice, as it were, in international agreements that involve provincial constitutional competences. This, too, would fall under the umbrella of reciprocal federalism.[3]

5: Summary

This full-blown version of ACCESS represents a thorough rethinking and reworking of the federal-provincial relationship within the federation. It is, however, the logical extension of the forces of globalization on the one hand and the recent federal initiatives on the social-policy/labour-market fronts on the other. And it resonates well with the written constitutional word. But the potential Achilles heel of the full-blown version of ACCESS is that the several embedded agreements or accords, whether interprovincial or federal-provincial, may not be binding on the parties. To this I now turn.

IV: COMPLIANCE, ENFORCEMENT AND REMEDIES

Designing an internal-union Convention that resonates well with governments and citizens will be difficult enough in its own right. Equally challenging will be to design processes of enforcement and dispute resolution that will likewise be deemed to be fair and acceptable. What follows are some tentative analyses relating to, first, ensuring compliance and enforcement and, second, providing fair and transparent dispute resolution and remedies.

A: Compliance and Enforcement

1: Can Ottawa Be Bound?

The appropriate starting point for the analysis of whether and how intergovernmental agreements can be made binding upon governments is the Supreme Court decision in the Canada Assistance Plan case. Since the issue at stake is steeped in Constitutional law, I shall defer to expert opinion here, namely Osgoode Hall Law School Professor Peter W. Hogg who also served as one of counsel to the Attorney General of Canada on this case. Hogg (1992, 307-8) summarizes the case as follows:

> In *Re Canada Assistance Plan* (1991), a constitutional challenge was made to a federal bill to implement a federal budget proposal that would place a five per cent annual cap on the growth of Canada Assistance Plan transfer payments from the federal government to the three provinces of Alberta, British Columbia and Ontario. (These three provinces were singled out because they were the three wealthiest provinces, as measured by their failure to qualify for equalization payments.) The Canada Assistance Plan (CAP) was a federal statute that authorized cost-sharing agreements be entered into by the federal government with the provinces, under which the federal government would undertake to pay 50 per cent of the costs incurred by the provinces in the provision of certain stipulated social assistance and welfare programmes. Under this authority, the federal government entered into CAP agreements with all ten provinces. By the terms of both the CAP legislation and each agreement, each agreement could be amended only with the consent of both the federal government and the province. It was argued that the budget proposal, by restricting the federal contributions to less than the agreed-upon 50 per cent share, was in effect a unilateral amendment of the three agreements which had not been made with the consent of the three affected provinces.
>
> While there was no doubt that the federal government was obliged to fulfil its side of the CAP arrangements so long as the CAP legislation remained unchanged, the effect of the proposed bill, once it was enacted, would be to amend the CAP legislation and thereby place a statutory limit on the federal government's CAP payments. Following the orthodox theory of parliamentary sovereignty, the Supreme Court of Canada held that Parliament remained free to amend the CAP legislation in this way (or in any other way) notwithstanding the cost-sharing agreements with the provinces.

However, all may not be lost since "while a legislative body is not bound by self-imposed restraints as to the *content, substance or policy* of its enactments, it is reasonably clear that a legislative body may be bound by *self-imposed procedural (or manner and form) restraints* on its enactments" (*Ibid*, 309, emphasis added). But this "manner and form restraint" did not apply in the Canada Assistance Plan case:

> The Court held that the consent [of the provinces] requirement was not a manner and form requirement for the simple reason that it expressly applied to the amendments to the agreements, not to the amendments of the legislation. Since the

legislation was silent on the question of the Parliament's power to enact new laws, that power was unimpaired, and could be used to alter the federal government's obligations under the agreements. The Court said that it would require a very clear indication in a statute, especially a non-constitutional statute, before the court would find an "intention of the legislative body to bind itself in the future." (*Ibid*, 313)

But even following the procedure in the last sentence of the quote may not do the trick, because it might run afoul of the rule that Parliament may not delegate its legislative powers to the provinces (Hogg, 1992, 313, note 55).

This creates real problems with the interim model outlined above and in particular with the notion that the announced $11 billion federal cash floor could ever be binding. In effect, the status quo would prevail: nothing now prevents the next budget, let alone the next Parliament, from reneging on this proposed floor. And unless the federal government were to embed this floor in manner and form legislation, it would likewise not be binding under the provisions of the interim model. And perhaps not even then.

Not surprisingly, therefore, the provinces (or at least some provinces) are pressing for a conversion of these cash transfers into tax-point transfers as the only sure way out of this dilemma. In this key area, these provinces would obviously prefer the full-blown ACCESS model to any version of an interim model. But this begs the further question: can interprovincial agreements be binding on the provinces?

2: Can Interprovincial Agreements Be Binding On the Provinces?

Not surprisingly, perhaps, the above concerns also arise in respect of intergovernmental agreements. In reference to the *Agreement On Internal Trade*, Katherine Swinton (1995, 199) offers the following observations:

> An agreement implemented through legislation that purports to impose binding obligations on the legislature remains, in a certain sense, unenforceable, because the doctrine of parliamentary sovereignty prevents a legislature from binding its successors, or even itself in the future, except through a formal constitutional amendment. Political accountability of the legislature to the current electorate takes precedence over ongoing adherence to past commitments or policy decisions. As a result, a legislature may unilaterally cancel its adherence to an intergovernmental agreement or legislate in defiance of its obligations in an implied repeal of its earlier adherence.

By way of an example, Swinton adds:

> [an] option for a government would be to pass legislation expressing a commitment to be bound by the recommendations of a dispute resolution panel.... But even if a

jurisdiction committed itself to be bound, this would be technically ineffective if the panel's decision required legislative action, such as the repeal or amendment of a standard or regulation, that a legislature were unwilling to undertake. Again, the principle of parliamentary supremacy ensures that the ultimate decision about whether to take legislative action remains with the legislature, not with the panel (Swinton, *op cit.*, 207).

There may, however, be creative ways around this problem. Some rest with the way in which the legislation is framed and executed. Others relate to the fact that these agreements are also political documents involving rights of citizens which in turn can make these documents binding politically, if not constitutionally. In pursuing these approaches, it is instructive to begin with the way in which the Australians have been able to make their intergovernmental agreements binding.

3: The Australian Model

Australia does not face the same problems as Canada in terms of making inter-state (interprovincial, in our terms) agreements binding. This is because their Constitution contains a provision for delegating powers upward. Specifically, s. 51(xxxvii) of the Australian Constitution reads:

51. The Parliament shall, subject to the Constitution, have power to make laws for the peace, order and good government of the Commonwealth with respect to

...

(xxxvii) Matters referred to the Parliament of the Commonwealth by the Parliament or Parliaments of any State or States, but so that the law shall extend only to States by whose Parliaments the matter is referred, or which afterwards adopt the law.

The best example of this relates to the recent Mutual Recognition Agreement among the states pertaining to regulations and standards relating to the sale of goods and the registration of occupations. (Note that the latter is an integral component of the proposed "full" ACCESS model.) The states designed the appropriate legislation, but then realized that this might not be binding on the various states. The solution became obvious: ask the Commonwealth to pass the identical legislation, after which the states would follow suit. Because of federal paramountcy in the Australian Constitution, the provision became binding — in effect constitutionalized.

Sturgess (1993, 10) elaborates on this process as follows:

...the Commonwealth is obtaining no power from the States under this very limited reference, other than to pass a single Act of Parliament once-for-all. It cannot pass further legislation in the same area, nor can it establish a bureaucracy through which to regulate the States. In that sense, there is no reference to *powers* at all.

In effect, the States are using the Commonwealth to jointly make an amendment to each of their constitutions at the one time. In practice, what the States are doing is ceding sovereignty to each other [and not to the Commonwealth — TJC].

This option is not available in Canada, clearly a shortcoming of our Constitution. For example, the Ontario desire to transfer securities regulation upward could easily be accommodated by such a route — Ottawa would pass legislation (perhaps drafted by the province(s)) and those provinces who then passed parallel legislation would be bound by it. Because this is not possible, Canada has to resort to other options.

4: *Creative Approaches to Ensuring Compliance*

With this as backdrop, one can now contemplate approaches that should go a long way to ensure that agreements, whether interprovincial or federal-provincial, can become effectively binding, albeit not constitutionalized.

The first approach draws from both the Australian experience as well as the concept of "manner and form" legislation. The process would work as follows. The governments would design an accord or convention that they would then initial. Template legislation would then be drafted and passed in the legislatures of all signing parties. Embedded in this legislation would be manner and form requirements for amendment procedures relating both to the legislation itself and any future amendments. This may not be constitutionally binding, but derogations from it would become very difficult, particularly if the convention itself emdodied citizen rights.

This leads to the second and related approach. In order to become effectively binding, a convention need not have constitutional backing if it has substantial political backing. Swinton (1995, 209) makes this very point in connection with the AIT:

...the absence of coercion is not fatal to an agreement if it gains the necessary legitimacy among political actors and citizens. One way to make the agreement more effective without changing the overall structure dramatically is to try to improve the effectiveness of the political process by emphasizing openness and accountability.

While not in any way tending to downplay the importance of the AIT, the fact of the matter is that the citizen appeal with respect to the economic union is likely to be minimal compared to the appeal that a convention on the social union or a convention guaranteeing free flow of occupational training across provinces. In other words, the pressures on all governments to abide by the provisions of conventions in these areas will be intense, if not overwhelming. And as Swinton has pointed out, if the processes are open and accountable then compliance is further guaranteed.

The third element of securing compliance is that the process will be aided by precedence and even the Constitution. Again, Swinton's comments are appropriate (and again she is referring to the AIT):

> Even without those mechanisms [constitutionalization — TJC], however, the Agreement on Internal Trade is likely to have an impact on Canadian law and government policy. Most of its effects will come because governments feel an obligation to comply, whether or not they have a legal ability to do otherwise. Over time, as well, the agreement may also filter into Canadian constitutional law, as courts use the principles to develop jurisprudence under the guarantee of labour mobility in section 6 of the Charter. (1995, 209)

In terms of the social union and the free flow of occupational standards this observation may be particularly telling.

Fourth, if the proposals for a full-blown ACCESS model come to fruition, this could include an enhanced s.121 of the Constitution which, in turn, will reinforce the observations in the previous point. One can surmise that many of the internal union provisions embodied in the various accords would eventually acquire constitutional status via this route. But even if the enhanced s.121 is not enshrined, the fact that it is included in the Convention (and, therefore, legislated by all parties) will influence the interpretation of the existing s.121.

Fifth, and finally, the degree of compliance on the part of governments will depend on the remedies associated with any derogations. As the recent Alberta health controversy has shown, citizens of the province do not want their governments to be offside with the provisions of the Canada Health Act. The issue is not one of dollars, but rather one of having the system declare that their government is pursuing policies that run counter to the national norms. Under the conventions contemplated in the full-blown ACCESS model, the remedies could go much further than a public announcement that government x or y is running afoul of nationally agreed-upon norms. It could involve expulsion from the internal union so that the mobility provisions no longer apply to the residents of the province. If this were part of the convention, then compliance would be virtually assured.

In summary, while interprovincial or federal-provincial conventions may not be legally or constitutionally binding, it nonetheless seems apparent that they can be given standing that makes derogations from the convention extremely difficult and, indeed, unlikely. To be sure, this depends in part on the specific guarantees embodied in the convention. But it is hard to conceive of federal-provincial and interprovincial agreements that would have to go through the open processes of ratification by the respective legislatures that would not be very appealing to Canadians.

B: Monitoring and Dispute Resolution

A key component in any federal-provincial or interprovincial agreement involves the on-going monitoring of the agreement and, when disputes arise as they obviously will, ACCESS to a transparent and fair dispute-resolution mechanism. These are not unfamiliar to Canadians and their governments: they exist under GATT and now the WTO; they exist under the FTA and NAFTA and they also are an integral part of the *Agreement on Internal Trade*. In terms of the AIT, which is essentially a convention in the way that I am using the term in this paper (although the Convention would also incorporate the social union and mutual recognition of skills accreditation), several analysts have focussed on the various ways in which the monitoring and dispute resolution mechanisms fall short of the ideal (e.g., Howse, 1995). And in an important sense this is certainly true, as will be elaborated later. However, as an entree to this section of the paper, I much prefer the more optimistic assessment and perspective of the AIT provided by Patrick Monahan (1995, 217). (In reading this quote, readers may wish to associate the references to the AIT with the social union and mutual recognition):

> Despite some not trivial shortcomings — both in the institutional provisions and elsewhere — the Agreement on Internal Trade nevertheless holds the potential to significantly reduce existing barriers to internal free trade in Canada. This potential lies not so much in any particular provision of the agreement, but in the recognition that internal trade in Canada ought to be subject to a set of binding norms. For the first time, governments in Canada have committed themselves to resolving trade disputes through a set of generally acceptable and enforceable rules. International experience with the General Agreement on Tariffs and Trade has shown that this commitment to a rules-based regime represents the fundamental breakthrough in promoting freer trade. Once a rules-based regime has been established — even if the substantive requirements of the rules are initially quite modest — a foundation has been laid for future construction.
>
> This is the promise and the potential of the Agreement on Internal Trade. Shot through with exceptions, caveats and reservations, it nevertheless commits governments to a set of norms for resolving trade disputes. It establishes a new set of political understandings about the extent to which governments should be allowed to discriminate against other Canadians in order to favour local or regional interests. In this relatively modest way, the agreement has the potential to counteract centrifugal

political forces that pose a continuing challenge to Canadian unity. The agreement reflects a belief, however tentative, in the primacy of Canadian citizenship and identity over local attachments. Because the obligations set out in the agreement are reciprocal and are to be enforced though a process that is transparent and fair, it represents one of the few politically acceptable avenues by which Canadian attachments can be permitted to prevail over local or provincial ones. In a country as fractious as Canada, that is no small achievement.

With this perspective, namely that the glass is half full rather than half empty, the further challenge is to design an approach to monitoring and dispute resolution that serves to fill the glass, as it were, and to convert the Convention into an integral substantive and symbolic institution of Canadian nationhood and identity. Without becoming overly involved in the institutional structure of the Convention, the following aspects would appear to have considerable merit:

- As already exists under the AIT, the extended Convention (AIT plus the social union and mutual recognition), will involve ad hoc working groups from the parties whose responsibility, among others, will be to design a set of operational guidelines based on the principles in the Convention. By their very nature, these guidelines will be subject to further refinement and elaboration as the Convention is implemented and wrestles with the complexities that will follow the implementation. Whether or not "stakeholders" are part of this initial process is not as important as making these guidelines public and allowing open processes for their evolution.

- As part of the Convention, there will have to be public administration with an appeal process. For purposes of expositional convenience, I shall associate this with the existence of an ombudsperson in each province (and one for the federal governement, where relevant). This becomes important since it is part of the institutional design whereby citizens can ACCESS the dispute resolution process directly. This would be an improvement over the AIT, where citizens who wish to launch a complaint must first attempt to persuade a government to bring the complaint on their behalf. Although the signatories to the Convention are governments, the Convention is really all about citizen rights in the socio-economic arena so that they must have independent and direct ACCESS.

- The complaint/appeal process might work as follows. Claims brought forward by a government or a citizen or a corporation would go through an initial screening group, which could be the group of ombudspersons or a separate screening panel as part of the Convention secretariat (which is called for under the AIT in any event). The role of the screening panel will be to either reject these appeals (e.g., because they are frivolous or because there is no obvious violation of the operational guidelines) or pass them onwards to the Conference secretariat. Initially, there may well be a flood of appeals, but as the operational guidelines become established and understood and as the rulings of the dispute-resolution committee interpret these guidelines, the screening exercise will become rather straightforward, if not easy.

• Complaints passed upwards by the screening panel, whether emanating from governments or citizens, will then end up in the first of two potential dispute resolution mechanisms, namely the political mechanism. At this political level, governments would be encouraged to explore compromise solutions or alternatives in response to the complaint. One would expect that most complaints would be resolved at this level, especially after the rulings of the formal dispute resolution mechanism become rather predictable.

• If the political mechanism cannot sort out the impasse, then the complaint would go the "administrative law" route to the dispute-resolution panel. Under the AIT provisions, a panel of 5 would be struck from the permanent roster of 65 experts to be maintained by the parties. One could imagine one panellist being selected by the challenger, one by the challenged govern-ment and three by the Convention secretariat. The panel's decision would become binding on the Convention.

• There would need to be some time frame within which the dispute must be resolved. One alternative here is to presume, for complaints that have gone beyond the screening process, that the claims or appeals will be accepted unless the process renders a negative decision within a specified timetable. In normal circumstances, this would mean placing the burden of proof on the government or governments to defend their barriers or impediments to the internal common market. This resonates well with the ACCESS acronym.

These are hardly firm proposals but are rather in the nature of a set of appropriate incentives to be embedded within the monitoring and dispute resolution aspects of the Convention.

At this point, it is useful to bring the earlier enforcement analysis into the picture. Suppose that the expert dispute-resolution panel recommends that prov-ince X rescind some particular legislative provision? Can the offending province (or Ottawa) refuse to go along with the recommendation? Constitutionally, the answer may well be yes, as suggested in the previous section. In practice, how-ever, this will be an implausible, if not impossible, result. There are several rea-sons for this. The first is that all parties would have passed the template legisla-tion creating the legislation is the first place. Hence they have voluntarily committed themselves to the system. The only way to not rescind the offending legislative provision is, in effect, to pull out of the Convention. The second, and related, reason follows on from the first. Withdrawal implies that a province's citizens no longer have the socio-economic rights under the Convention. Nor does its business sector have the Convention's protection in terms of ACCESSing the internal market. Thus, refusing to abide by the panel's recommendation would involve an enormous political and economic cost. Third, the Convention is likely to become very popular and the recommendations of the dispute-resolution panel will likely also receive strong popular support especially if the process is "transparent and fair", to use Monahan's words. In other words, while ACCESS may be difficult to bring to fruition, it will be much more difficult to unwind, once in place.

By way of a final comment on the design of the convention for a full-blown ACCESS model, it is clear that this institution will constrain Parliamentary flexibility, even sovereignty. Indeed, this is the *raison d'être* of such a Convention — in effect it is a set of social and economic rights of citizens and private-sector agents generally. As a result, aspects of sovereignty will become shared among the provinces and Ottawa or, if one prefers, transferred to the new institutional Convention. Perhaps an even better way to express the result is that sovereignty will be transferred to individual Canadians. In any event, there is no free lunch for governments here. But this is increasingly what globalization is all about — a mushrooming array of international and domestic "contracts" among governments and between governments and private sector agents in the trade, military, environmental, economic, etc., areas. As globalization proceeds, sovereignty inevitably becomes more diffused and dispersed. Indeed, with or without the Convention, citizens/corporations will gain guaranteed ACCESS to the internal union, so that the real issue becomes one of whether ACCESS is preferable to the range of other options for securing the internal market.

V: PROCESS

As the final substantive section of this paper, it is appropriate to devote some attention to process or, more specifically, to focus on how ACCESS might come to fruition.

The answer in terms of the interim model seems perfectly clear. Essentially, all it would take would be some initial moves by Ottawa and in particular a federal commitment to place the oversight and policing role of the CHST cash transfers at the service of a federal-provincial monitoring and enforcement agency. The rest of the interim model would then quickly fall into place. This relates to the earlier claim that the interim model is capable of immediate implementation.

Triggering the full-blown ACCESS model is a more difficult process challenge. However, it seems clear that the provinces would have to take the lead role. Specifically, one way would be to convert the principles in their *Report to Premiers* into a workable interprovincial accord on the social union. They will also have to design a mutual-recognition accord for skills transferability and they will probably have to undertake something more than a best-efforts approach to implementing the provisions of the AIT. Beyond all of this, they will probably have to commit themselves to a Convention embodying all of this as well as an appropriate enforcement and dispute-resolution mechanism. But if they can accomplish this, then the pressure for compliance falls on Ottawa. If the internal socioeconomic union is secured, there is no longer any rationale for federal cash transfers to the provinces as an enforcing mechanism. Hence, this current rationale is no longer a stumbling block in terms of converting cash transfers to tax-point transfers. And the dynamics underlying the CHST and the transfer of training to the provinces means that the logical and consistent next step is for Ottawa to allow UI to be more accommodative of provincial policies to forge an integration of the entire labour-market/education/welfare subsystem. Given that the status quo is hardly a fall back position, Ottawa will have difficulty holding out, particularly if citizens embrace the "national" initiatives of the provinces. Indeed, if the process gets rolling, Ottawa will likely come in at an early stage to press its own interests.

The previous sentence is more revealing than it might at first appear. Essentially, the view of the federal government and, I suspect, the view of Canadians generally, is that the provinces will never get their act together, i.e., they will never subject their "provincial " interests to the national interest and, therefore, the attempt at creating a workable Convention will come to naught. As long as this perception prevails, the federal government presumes that it can count on citizen support for a strong central role, even a unilateral central role, in monitoring and policing the internal socio-economic union. This is a very questionable presumption on Ottawa's part, since the vacuum left by the disappearing status quo is quickly and surprisingly coming to be filled by creative provincial initiatives.

This leads to my final observation on process. What the Australian experience with mutual recognition has revealed is that the exercise quickly becomes dynamically attractive. Essentially, the provisions for mutual recognition were developed by three of the six Australian states. Once the process became well launched, however, citizens of other states effectively demanded that their own states also sign on. Carried over to the Canadian scene, the real challenge becomes one of finding four or five provinces to begin the process of developing principles and legislation for securing the socio-economic union. At this point, the process will develop a dynamic that will virtually ensure that all other provinces will come on board: their citizens will settle for nothing less. This process may not generate the "Charter" fever of the early 1980s, but it may come close. Thus Ottawa will have to come on board as well.

In terms of the process dimension of the full-blown ACCESS model, the initial challenge is not to approach the exercise by insisting on bringing all ten provinces on board all at once. Rather, the key may well be for four or five like-minded provinces to begin the process of design and implementation of the socio-economic Convention and then let "contagion" do the rest.

VI: CONCLUSION

Decentralization is a reality. Powers are in the process of being devolved. More ominously, financial responsibility, especially in the social policy arena, is also being devolved to the provinces. As a result, the federal-provincial economic and financial interface is in full evolutionary flight — there is no status quo.

This is an unacceptable situation for a country which has long taken pride in its comprehensive east-west social contract. Canada and Canadians need to reconstitute and revitalize our socio-economic union. The role of this paper is to serve as a catalyst in this process. The analysis focussed on two alternative (although presumably time-consistent) approaches to a socio-economic Convention. One (the interim ACCESS model) is more federal-provincial in nature whereas the full-blown ACCESS model is more interprovincial and, I think, more in line both with the letter of the Constitution and with the manner in which the federal-provincial interface is evolving. And between these two versions is no doubt a continuum of alternative models.

One of the contributions of the above analysis is that the full ACCESS model represents a real, live option. While not constitutionally "air-tight" (nor is the interim model for that matter) the full-blown ACCESS Convention is eminently achievable and the dispute-resolution systems are likely to be workable and enforceable on the parties. As a result, there is in effect a rich menu of alternative approaches to reconstituting our social-economic union and plenty of room for strategic bargaining and negotiation on the part of both orders of government.

This, then, leads to the *raison d'être* of the paper — to challenge all governments to move quickly in this area of preserving and promoting Canada's internal socio-economic union, keeping in mind that the name of the game, above all else, is to endow Canadians with a guaranteed set of rights and privileges on the socio-economic front. No doubt many readers will view the full ACCESS model as embodying a degree of decentralization that they are not comfortable with. If the comparison is traditional post-war status quo, then their concerns are probably warranted. With respect, however, this is coming at the underlying issue from precisely the wrong direction. The reality is that Canada is undergoing unprecedented decentralization — some of it driven by global forces and some of it policy- and fiscal-driven. From this perspective, ACCESS acquires a quite different rationale, namely, how in the face of this decentralization do we maintain the integrity of our social and economic union? ACCESS may not be the answer, but Canadians must surely devise some reasonable facsimile that challenges the provinces to shoulder enhanced "pan-Canadian" responsibilities commensurate with their increased powers.

NOTES

I wish to thank Richard Simeon, Katherine Swinton and analysts from the Ontario Ministry of Intergovernmental Affairs for valuable comments on an earlier draft. However, responsibility for the ideas expressed in the paper rest entirely with the author.

1. Note that I am using "standstill" in its trade-agreement context, i.e., no deregotations from the existing degree of interprovincial mobility or from existing principles. The standstill provision is not about provincial evolution of various policy areas. Indeed, under the former CAP provisions, there was no requirement that a province even have a welfare program, so that it is not appropriate to view standstill as relating to the status quo of any individual program.
2. This is not quite correct. There will still be a very important federal presence in most of these areas where truly national issues are at stake. Consider health, for example; Ottawa would continue to control/monitor key areas such as drug accreditation, national blood monitoring systems, etc., as well as the interaction between health and immigration. What the statement in the text is meant to imply is that, in the day-to-day relationship between individuals and the health care system, the provinces will be paramount.
3. This concern that creative arrangements be put in place to ensure that Canada can speak with one voice with respect to international treaties in areas of exclusive provincial jurisdiction is also addressed in Burelle (1995).

REFERENCES

Burelle, André (1995) *Le mal canadien: essai de diagnostic et esquisse d'une thérapie* (Montreal: Fides).

Burelle, André (1996) "A Renewed Canada Should Say Yes", *Canada Opinion* vol. 4, No. 1 (Ottawa: Council for Canadian Unity).

Courchene, Thomas J. (1994) *Social Canada in the Millennium: Reform Imperatives and Restructuring Principles* (Toronto: C.D. Howe Institute).

Courchene, Thomas J. (1996) "Revitalizing and Rebalancing Canadian Federalism: In Quest of a New National Policy", prepared for the Canadian Political Science Association Conference *After the Referendum: What is the Path Ahead* (Ottawa, January 26-28, 1996), forthcoming in Conference volume.

Courchene, Thomas J. (1996a) *Macro Federalism: Some Exploratory Research Relating to Theory and Practice* (Washington, D.C.: The World Bank), forthcoming.

Greenspon, Edward (1996) "Jobs Spotlight On Provinces, Young Says", *The Globe and Mail* (August 7), A4.

Group of 22 (1996) *Making Canada Work Better*

Hogg, Peter W. (1992) *Constitutional Law of Canada* 3rd edition (Scarborough: Carswell).

Howse, Robert (1995) "Between Anarchy and the Rule of Law: Dispute Settlement and Related Implementation Issues in the Agreement on Internal Trade" in Michael Trebilcock and Daniel Schwanen (eds.) *Getting There: An Assessment of the Agreement on Internal Trade* (Toronto: C.D. Howe Institute), pp. 170-195.

Ministerial Council on Social Policy Reform and Renewal (1995) *Report to Premiers* (mimeo).

Monahan, Patrick J. (1995) "To the Extent Possible: A Comment on Dispute Settlement in the Agreement on Internal Trade" in Michael Trebilcock and Daniel Schwanen (eds.) *Getting There: An Assessment of the Agreement on Internal Trade* (Toronto: C.D. Howe Institute), pp. 211-218.

Ontario Economic Council (1983) *A Separate Personal Income Tax For Ontario: An Ontario Economic Council Position Paper* (Toronto: OEC).

Sargent, Timothy C. (1995) "An Index of Unemployment Insurance Disincentives", Working Paper No. 95-10 (Ottawa: Finance Canada).

Sturgess, Gary L. (1993) "Fuzzy Law and Low Maintenance Regulation: The Birth of Mutual Recognition in Australia" paper prepared for a Conference on Mutual Recognition sponsored by the Royal Institute of Public Administration (Brisbane, February 12), mimeo.

Swinton, Katherine (1995) "Law, Politics, and the Enforcement of the Agreement on Internal Trade" in Michael Trebilcock and Daniel Schwanen (eds.) *Getting There: An Assessment of the Agreement on Internal Trade* (Toronto: C.D. Howe Institute), pp. 196-210.

Thurow, Lester (1993) "Six Revolutions, Six Economic Challenges", *Toronto Star* (January 28, p.A.21).

Zuker, Richard (1995) "Reciprocal Federalism: Beyond the Spending Power" (mimeo).

Contributors

André Burelle Former senior constitutional advisor to the Trudeau and Mulroney governments, author of *Le Mal Canadien.*

David Cameron Professor, Department of Political Science, University of Toronto.

Thomas J. Courchene, Jarislowsky-Deutsch Professor of Economic and Financial Policy; Director, John Deutsch Insitute for the Study of Economics, Queen's University.

Roger Gibbins Professor, Department of Political Science, University of Calgary.

Gordon Gibson Senior Fellow, Fraser Institute, Vancouver.

Peter Leslie Professor, Department of Political Studies, Queen's University.

David Milne Professor, Department of Political Science, University of Prince Edward Island.

Katherine Swinton Professor, Faculty of Law, University of Toronto.